Affirmation

A Bilingual Anthology, 1919–1966

D1263198

Affirmation

A Bilingual Anthology, 1919-1966

BY JORGE GUILLÉN

Translated, with Notes, by Julian Palley
Introduction by Jorge Guillén

University of Oklahoma Press
Norman

By Julian Palley

La luz no usada: La poesía de Pedro Salinas (Studium,
    Mexico, 1966)
Affirmation: A Bilingual Anthology (Norman, 1968)

*The paper on which this book is printed bears the watermark
    of the University of Oklahoma Press and is designed for
    an effective life of at least three hundred years.*

International Standard Book Numbers:
    0–8061–0764–2 (cloth); 0–8061–0940–8 (paper)

Library of Congress Catalog Card Number: 68–15667

To Shirley

Preface

Posterity, if it comes upon the great resounding Yes of
Cántico *among the tumbled fragments of our time, will*
not believe that No was all we had to answer to the world.
—ARCHIBALD MacLEISH

JORGE GUILLÉN belongs to that remarkable generation of Spanish poets, the "Generation of 1927," as it is called, that boasted Federico García Lorca, Rafael Alberti and Pedro Salinas. A generation that was dispersed, nearly in its entirety, by the Civil War and the Franco victory. García Lorca was shot by the rebels; Alberti went into exile to Argentina; Salinas and Guillén, exiles also, came to teach in American universities. Salinas and Guillén were from the northern provinces, from Castile, old and new; Lorca and Alberti are both Andalusians. Their poetry, in a broad sense, reflects their regions. Beside the Andalusian folkloric motifs and rich, exuberant imagery of Lorca and Alberti, the poetry of Guillén and Salinas seems to be rooted in the austere, often bare tableland of the Castiles, the homeland of great mystics like Santa Teresa de Avila and San Juan de la Cruz, where the high *meseta* seems close to the sky. There is a like austerity in Guillén's poetry; it does not appeal immediately to the senses. Its real fervor and passion are contained in the molds of classical forms; the complexity of imagery and metaphor require the intellectual collaboration of the reader, a collaboration that is repaid abundantly by the intensity of the artistic experience.

Jorge Guillén was born in Valladolid on the eighteenth of January, 1893. He studied in Switzerland and Madrid, and received the master's degree from the University of Granada in 1913. He was in Germany during 1913–14, and was a lecturer in Spanish at the Sorbonne from 1917 to 1923. In 1924 he received his doctorate from the University of Madrid. He began the writing of *Cán-*

tico in 1919, in the village of Tregastel, Brittany. Guillén taught at Murcia from 1925 to 1928, at Oxford University from 1929 to 1931, then at the University of Seville until 1938. Since 1938 he has resided in the United States, and is now retired from Wellesley College, where he taught until 1957.

In 1921 Guillén married Germaine Cahen, who died in 1947. In 1961 he was married to Irene Mochi Sismondi, in Bogotá. He makes extended visits to Europe, especially to Italy. His friendship with Pedro Salinas, who died in 1951, was profound and lasting.

Until recently, Guillén was the author of a single book of poetry, *Cántico*, that appeared in four successive and augmented editions, those of 1928, 1936, 1945, and 1950. This last edition, the first complete *Cántico*, appeared in Buenos Aires. There followed *Clamor*, in three parts: *Maremágnum* (1957), *... Que van a dar en la mar* (1960), and *A la altura de las circunstancias* (1963). *Homenaje*, the last part of *Aire Nuestro*, his life work, appeared in 1967.

Cántico, in its near exclusion of historical and social themes, approaches the ideal of "pure poetry," or, as Guillén has said, *Poesía pura, ma non troppo*. Its poetry is concerned with the celebration of Being, the moment caught in its elusiveness, a Spring day with poplars, love, and the problem of death. It is a hymn, a canticle to the joy of being alive. Few poets of our time have sung so perfectly and fervently their acceptance of Being. *Clamor* seemed at first to be a divergence from this goal of pure poetry. But as its three volumes appeared, it became increasingly clear that *Cántico* and

Clamor represents a unity, in spite of the surface differences, a single and harmonious expression of the poet's art and thought. If it is true that *Cántico* tends toward poetic purity and an affirmative, joyous view of life, and that *Clamor* emphasizes social criticism and the disquietudes of our civilization, it is also true that there are moments of anguish and *poésie engagée* in *Cántico*, although they are in the background—minor, subdued themes, overshadowed by the book's praise of Being. Nor can it be denied that there are moments of wholeness and joy in *Clamor*, as is testified by the final verses of *El acorde*, the initial poem of *Maremágnum*. Moments of plenitude and joy, and, above all, poems of human affirmation. Indeed, "La afirmación humana" is the title of Guillén's moving tribute to Anne Frank (from *A la altura de las circunstancias*), in whose tragedy the poet sees a symbol of man's affirmation in the face of overwhelming adversity. And all of his work is an attempt to reach that "difficult humanity" of which he speaks in "Despertar español" ("Spanish Awakening"):

> *A través de un idioma*
> *¿Yo podría llegar a ser el hombre*
> *Por fin humano a que mi esfuerzo tiende*
> *Bajo este sol de todos?*
>
> (With the aid of my language
> could I aspire to be that man
> at last human toward whom my hand reaches
> beneath this common sun?)

Human affirmation and an attempt to reach a condition

of authentic humanity, these are the goals of our Castilian poet; and if, in *Cántico,* he sought these goals primarily through purity, intensity of vision and exclusion, in *Clamor* he seeks them through commitment, through an embrace, a going-out, an assumption of responsibility for the multitude of man's evils. This later effort has demanded a modification of the brilliant metaphors and classicism of *Cántico*—a step toward easier communication and overt statement—but it is for this no less praiseworthy, and no less successful.

Homenaje, the final part of *Aire Nuestro,* is a collection of pieces alluding to specific persons, glosses and comments on writers of the near and distant past, epistles in verse, translations from English, French, Italian, and German, and poems in which Guillén looks back gratefully, but with a gentle sadness, at his long and eventful life, in verses that have lost none of their power and beauty: "The Earth is a great adventure" concludes one of the last poems. Turning away from the history and social problems of *Clamor, Homenaje* is a homage to the universal literary tradition to which he belongs, to friends and family, and to that flow, that Being, of which he is a "spark."

In poetry in general, and especially in Guillén's poetry, sound and sense are inseparable. The more closely a translator approaches the meaning of a poem, so much must he sacrifice its music; and as he approximates, in another tongue, the sound of the original, its cadence and rhyme, to a similar degree the meaning becomes obscured. This translator has tried to walk the narrow line between sound and sense, trying to give its due to both, but at times, inevitably, sacrificing one to the other. It is hoped that some of the translations have value as poetry, but they are intended primarily as a guide to the originals.

I am most grateful for the generous and painstaking help received from Jorge Guillén in the preparation of this anthology. Much of whatever value this work may have is due to this close collaboration between poet and translator. Don Jorge has read nearly every word of the translations and notes, and the editor has benefited from his extensive and acute comments. Still, errors creep in, and for those I claim exclusive credit.

My sincere thanks also to Professor Ivar Ivask, editor of *Books Abroad,* for helpful suggestions in the final preparation of the manuscript.

JULIAN PALLEY

Contents

xiv

Affirmation

A Bilingual Anthology, 1919–1966

Introduction

This Introduction is a translation, by the editor, of "El argumento de la obra," *an essay by Jorge Guillén which was published in book form by All'Insegna del Pesce D'Oro, Milan, 1961*—Translator's note.

·

I

L<small>IGHT</small>! It invades / all my being. Wonder!" These verses—which belong to the first stanza of the first poem in the first part of *Cántico*—sum up the initial fact that opens the door to the world expressed by this work: the dawn together with the act of awakening. Light is reborn. It is reborn in the eyes and mind of a man moved by the fundamental emotion of wonder. Thus this man is able to know himself, thanks to the contact with a *beyond* different from himself. The subject—the "I"—would be nothing were it not for that net of relations with the object, with objects. They are there, by themselves, and before themselves, autonomous, and with one supreme quality: they are real. The awakening of each sleeper re-establishes the confrontation that is our life: an "I" in dialogue with reality. The "I" is imprisoned in something infinitely superior to itself, and by chance stroke of an involuntary, and most fortunate, player. From this, his wonder. "For me, for my wonder, / all is greater than I." The world is esteemed because it is, it is there, it really exists, because it is real. To this basic virtue can be added innumerable traits, pro and con. Beneath this light of dawning it is only this clash—physical and metaphysical—that matters.

The surrounding world appears and reappears as a gift for the creature, infinitely enriched. The supreme bond of presence: "I am, I am ... How? With you, / World with you!" No, one cannot believe in solitude as a desirable category. A man says to the world: "May there be always / your absolute company." *Cántico*

3

is above all a canticle to that essential company. Whoever lives it is never isolated. (Not even his individual ways will be manifested or intervene.) This actor would be nothing without his scenery. "I am rich / from so much treasured Creation!" Consequently: "Thus I am profoundly, I know myself / thanks to you, who exist." The imperative—vital and ethical—has to be: "Into the thicket!" Let us enter further into the mass of being, of the beings who are there. "To be more, to be intensely and now . . ." It is the human task. One must maintain and increase this privilege of being among beings, participating in their plenitude.

Everything springs from that primordial intuition. A mind awakens in a context of harmony. Of course, this relation occurs only between a man beyond his chaos and a world beyond its chaos. When health and freedom are sufficient, man affirms himself by affirming Creation, thus capitalized. He who is thus affirmed must conclude joyously humble: "I depend on things!" He is humble, or rather, placed within his context, between accepted limits and always with reference to a Whole. Terrestrial man loves the "holy earth" that he treads. "Thus, walking, I enjoy / a better being . . . / on possessed realities." Realities which, for their part, possess the possessor, who knows nothing of existence on a solitary island. He will always find himself embraced to the Other. "Is it not I whom he discovers?" Ineluctable alliance: "I am nothing without you, world." During this flash of capital intuition, one could not assert: I am. There is only possible, fortunately, a "we are." And that isn't all. When the mind registers being, it evaluates it,

and if the mind is not greatly perturbed, Being is identi-
fied with the Good in a satisfactory manner. "And
nothing more: to be. / It is enough. Its joy is /absolute"
—a joy which would be meaningless in an isolated being.
It exists in the astonished meeting: the subject is united
with "An absolute existence / situated in an abrupt /
Beyond." Such a situation is expressed by the formula:
"We are, therefore we matter." (*Somos, luego valemos.*)
From this sort of *cogito*—not an idea, but an intuition in
its origin—there derives this *Cántico* and, perhaps, every
canticle. We awaken, we are, we are together. Man appears thus, co-partner in a universal value, and his part
will always be smaller than that of the Other.

There is no room for the exaltation of the "I." "We
are worthy" if we share this good, common to all who
exist. The original intuition is not felt only by him who
is granted certain prerogatives. There is no mystical ec-
stasy. No experience could be more normal—so normal
that we forget it. We go through our days without think-
ing about this base which sustains us. There are moments of interruption. Then we are aware of the equilibrium that unites our ordinary lives to our ordinary
surroundings. It is as if nothing were happening. Nothing? Only an ordering of forces which are combined
with incredible success. The human animal manages,
up to a certain point, to fit into his environment, and
that adjustment between the eyes and light, between the
lungs and air, between feet and the earth implies a co-
ordination so obvious that often the most attentive do
not perceive it. This harmony does not reach their ears.
And yet, nothing is superior to our familiar equilibrium.

Well may it be called a marvel. "I believe in the sufficient marvel / of this street at eleven / when life grows strong / with normal vitality . . ." *Cántico* attends to those instants when nothing occurs but the extraordinary phenomenon of normality. Adventures take place against its grey background. This precious grey possesses a serene vigor, a double, reciprocal vigor: "The wall gives more whiteness to my tranquil eyes." The white wall calms the seer, who, for his part, doubles that whiteness with the tranquility of his look. Let us not think of an esthetic act, out-of-the-ordinary. Life functions as usual. Conclusion: "All obliges me to be the center of the equilibrium."

6

The "center" belongs to anyone, and is found in any place. "Where to go astray, where? / My center is this point: Anywhere. So replete / The world always awaits me." It is a world without voids that never becomes emptiness. "There is so much reality manifest!" At least it is true now, with this relative abundance. Later there will be severances and negations. Now the things are imposing themselves, when—full of themselves—they are what they are. "A tranquility / of constant affirmation / guides all beings." Among them and with them, man affirms them and affirms himself, and not by logical sequence. "Affirmation which is hunger: my instinct always right!" Instinct, elemental impulse; from the body and its pulsations it rises to the surrounding atmosphere. "I am adjusted to my limits," which in a certain sense I shall transcend. "I am! / Of the wind, across the afternoon, more wind, / I am more than I myself!" No fusion, and no magic, but yes, the enrichment of him who lives exulting in his life. On these occasions there bursts from the depths of vitality, with the force of a jet of water, a physical and metaphysical joy, foundation now of an enthusiastic conviction, of a faith: faith in reality, in this terrestrial reality. "They are prodigies of the earth ...," and without mechanical tricks, and therefore more prodigious. "Oh Reality, finally / real, in apparition!" Things are revealing themselves. "Matter provides / the Grace of Apparition: this is mortar, this is wicker." Thus capitalized, Grace and Apparition are not meant to suggest a miracle. Is not the fulfillment of a natural law more surprising than its miraculous contraventions? "A balcony, the windows / some books, a table. / Nothing more? Yes, / concrete marvels." The eyes of the spirit are pleased to record compact objects, possessed of their own being, in harmony with their definition, faithful to their essence. "The detail has recourse to all its surroundings: / stones, this wall, a wire farther on." The surroundings distinguish and intensify that which it is. What matters is the plenitude of these realities, not their beauty. (Of course symmetry displays the object in its necessary splendor.) "Stone," "wall," "wire" evoke a modest portion of the planet. But they are exactly what they are. That's the *quid*.

II

Such an attitude demands a presence in space and the present in time. Presence brings with it the desired revelation, and the beyond becomes an irrefutable immediate limit. "Could I be worthy of their love: / volume, form, presence!" *Estar* (Being in a specific space and time) constitutes the consummation of *ser* (Being in the abstract). "You are. (*Eres*) Potential good fortune! / But even more: you are here and now (*estás*)." And he adds: "But it is not enough to be. / Alone, still dark / Who does not seek in presence / his illumination . . . ?" Yes, the "present form" gives us our "highest reality." Reality here—and now. The present is the least pathetic time. In the present one does not seek the tension of conflict, but the tension of union and fusion and the greatest boon. The Present "so elusive / in its marrow and pith" is that which offers "the utmost taste of life." Past and future remain in the latent state of ideas. Only the present is real, although the inattentive may not be sensitive to its pulsating and may judge to be intemporal that act which is "now" occurring. Since nothing is isolated, time is never a superficial phenomenon. "That which was, that which will be, /pulsate, immediate now." The present never stops flowing with the great continuous river.

On all sides one confronts the universe in its heights of abundance, of consistency, of health. Air and light as well constitute a most active background or medium. "There is no solitude. There is light everywhere. I am yours." And also: "I am; I am here and now. / I breathe the deepest air." We give thanks to this marriage of the air with our lungs, and the rhythm of *Cántico* follows the rhythm of our breathing. "I breathe, I believe." Man lives and survives according to the harmony—stronger than any chaos—between the habitant and his environment.

Through many months our terrestrial denizen knows dawns, mornings, noons, afternoons, sunsets, nights, springs, summers, autumns, winters, heat and cold, light and shadow, earth and sky—illuminated by the sun, the moon, the constellations. And beyond the found world, he knows the invented world: the city. They are "The interrupted solitudes," Nature's urban interludes. If the city is, on the other hand, a profusion of abuse and bustle, it represents, above all, the exaltation of human energy. "There floats a clamor / of efforts." "Tumult of inventions!" Energy is glorified, man's impulse to achieve authentic humanity. Beside the "illustrious shores" or the "great civil river of history," in the "City of summers" or of the "winters," one divines the "advent / of the gods of Now," of our contemporary civilization, which one must face up to in its inextricable confusion. "Live within me, great city! And such you are: Weigh upon me / with your illustrious gifts."

Significant also in a meridional city is the "Street of Dawn," "Humble eternity in a short byway." In the suburb, in an early "almost ugly light," work takes its place. "Light bulb / humble candle: holy vessel / for the working light." And in the factories: "The smoke pierces the air / through a valiant chimney," and the workers: "Dark folk: / coal against the blue." And there, in the poor suburb, the taverns: "The tinkling will sound / of copper / on / so much laminated zinc." Life always wants more life. Observe how "Four streets are tied together: / climax toward a stronger living." Aspiration toward construction: "Victory: fine unity" is obtained by the "Plaza Mayor," center of a system, an attempt which seeks its own beyond: "Thus, city, you prepare / to arrive at complete Being?" The human animal aspires to attain the state of manhood, to become a man within his community. "To lose oneself, / to become the crowd!" A common fatigue ties others to "The lost one among so many . . . ," fatigue or struggle. "Oh struggle amidst the bustle!" A pacific struggle amid the street bustle, which can become a celebration of communion: "Hubbub of the fiesta, / of a friendly warmth, / of people as a forest, / of smiles and glances . . . ." It is the people, "the compact people." And all is joined, / fecund."

That human interest, which before was collective, now focuses upon particular figures, above all in their springtime freshness: children, young women. (There are no old people in *Cántico*.) Friendship emerges as the most intense form of living together. "Friends: / two voices made equal." It is "A love which neither swears nor promises . . . ." The amicable sentiment embraces multitudes." "I am your *aficionado,* living beings." The most intimate persons are present also (father, mother, children). There is no life without hope, unless it is in the throes of death. "Let the dead bury their dead, / but touch not hope. / It is mine, it will be yours / here and for generations." All *Cántico* ascends toward love, and not because love is the principle which moves the sun and the other stars. Thanks to this accord we achieve reality's plenitude. "There overflows life's / greatest apogee." Thus is achieved, in its rigorous tension, the unity of soul and body. A great victory: the lovers "Deny chaos, overcome its assault," and in a real redoubt, without paradisiacal fictions. "Love without escape to paradise, / love rushing to the most precise / and real country, present and without outskirts." The Here and Now are obliged, by love, to surrender their greatest treasure. There surges and resurges—in a renascent song of songs —the act of love. "Joy of joys: the soul is on the skin . . . ." "Joy of being: / the love astonished." Now indeed the vital affirmation casts off any negative component: "Love is always life, life, life." Love as creation, and, above all, that of the lovers themselves: "You create us, Love, you, you love us." And as a result: "Through this joy, the world sheds / its disorder." Thus love is focused on its base, its critical moment: "Reality in action, / anguished, joyful, most perfect." In fine: "Body is soul, and all is union." And love realized shall be "Soul in its flesh: pure."

Among the works of men, some stand out that permit us to glimpse a kind of perfection that is attainable and attained, very different from an impossible, ideal perfection, far from any platonic archetype. The arts refine raw material. For example: gardens. "The grass / responds to our eyes and our feet / with the gentleness of that which has been worked." Among works of art a favored treatment is conceded to music. This "absolute harmony in human air" achieves a "culmination of reality" and becomes a "world." But the attraction of the masterwork never leads to a leisurely esthetic recreation. There are windows, and never an ivory tower. "Ivory? Glass. I retreat to no / rich refuge. / My defense is the glass / of a beloved window . . . ," a window open to ineluctable communication. Here is the satire of the esthete and his affectations, summed up by the color and word "amaranth." "Amaranth! Rounded and hermetic / paradises / always slightly smothered, / submarine, supercelestial, / in excessively vespertine hours / too gentle with fringes and murmurs." After this ironic rejection, there follows, with more general intent: "No, no! / Not so much paradise for a profane being. / The amaranth, no." What then? "The sea-air on land!" Our air, free air. Paradise appears neither as the nostalgia for a past nor as a desire for a future. *Cántico* presents reality only as it is. There is only the real candle, that which burns. Its fire lights up conditions which, by grateful hyperbole, are considered paradisiacal. In a garden, and before "a man—with his serene moment." Or in some childhood and its "gusts of paradise." Or in love. "Paradise that is he with her . . . ," their indubitable existence. Then as always can only be conceived and praised a "Love without escape to paradise . . . ." No escape, but immersion, rather, "Into the thickness!" in the thicknesses of things, in true profundity.

In this fashion, through accidents and uncertain movements, earth and the Earth are touched, and the order which makes it inhabitable is descried. In perpetual creation, everything relates to everything. "I believe in the most evident Creation," albeit it is perturbed by innumerable contradictions and catastrophes. But . . . "Such a moving bond—places me face to face with essences . . . ." Essences—existences. "I believe in a subtle / chorus, in that tacit / music beneath the confusion." No one can refuse the role of witness. "There was a witness of the immaculate blue." "Twelve o'clock, noon." The visible circle of the hours symbolizes the invisible total circle. "It was I, / center at that moment / of so much existence, / I, who saw all things / replete for a god." Creation reveals itself in such a way that one can postulate a possible path to a Creator. For the time being, we have before us the terrestrial presence. *Cántico* is limited to its exaltation.

III

Cántico assumes a relatively balanced relationship between a healthy and free protagonist and a world in which all is well. This kind of relationship, normal, shall we say, is subject (as we know very well) to crises. "How the human incident pullulates!" An accompaniment in chiaroscuro defines those correspondences. The background is in chiaroscuro. The attention converges toward the luminous, encircled center. Chance and disorder, evil and pain, time and death damage and overturn. They interfere even in the first dawn. "Noises interrupt . . . ." Then, in the city's afternoon, "Steps and shouts / confusedly arise . . . / music becomes noise." The noise becomes uproar, "A crash of struggle," of war, "men in emphatic clamor." Or of animals: "The night with its howling beasts arises." The enigma "As a wail in form of menace" is depicted by the "uproar," and also: "The monster strains and creaks noisily." In other words: a hubbub. "A hubbub / of noise inflamed." Worse still: "An anonymous something that buzzes and threatens." The adversary appears "In a mad, confused rush." They are confused, jumbled beings led blindly by chance. Only the overcoming of this blindness can explain the liveable world.

Of course chance can be fortunate, but it almost never has this meaning. "Winds, fertile chance, a bubbling of directions." "At the hands of chance" is produced rather a chaos. Fertile or sterile, it is often taken into reckoning. "Playing with hours / that play among / all the fortunes . . . ." One plays with life and death. "O void profile, / sketched by Chance!" is said of a cadaver. It happens that chance is dominant. "Diminutive passers-by / bind their chance / to the paths" of a city. At times chance is called "unruly," an instrument, perhaps, of Nothingness. "It is not, it will not be Nothingness. Will No-being dominate us / with the aid of that chance / hostile to every form?" Chance is anticreative. "If chance were not already my faith . . . ." One must be on one's guard in the face of that initiative. The musician, for example, should eliminate chance. "And thus, with implacable / solicitude, chance / so overcome . . . ." It is a state of warfare: chance will not dissolve into dissonances.

But, alas, it does so dissolve. The words that signify disorder are repeated: tumult, abuse, mob, discordance, confusion, disturbance, farrago, uproar, hubbub, hodgepodge, clamor. Such disorder, great or small, is not always harmful: "The sun-swept confusion" of a holiday morning. In the final analysis, there is a world when men "Deny chaos, conquer its threat." Such success is not always achieved. "Worse: the igniting of chaos." "Men there are that destroy, in wretched / disorder, their voices and their hearts."

The disorder is physical, also. "The atmosphere unravels: / Invisible in its useless fibre, / the object gives the lie to itself." This formless vagueness implies dissolution, although it may be reduced to a simple mist: "a still / modest chaos." That chaos of the great city is not so modest: "Contradiction, disorder, hubbub: / mob." The personage who says "I" is also part of the crowd. "Oh multitude, also mine, / that I am also!" I, or that is, "One among many." Or: "Man. / You? And I also. Everyone. / Confusion, crime, quarrelling." Social disorder extends to delinquency. "So many men and together? / I know: varied the lies / in these streets, and less varied the crime." A disorder which can put the earth itself into mortal danger: "Through angry repeated clashes, / mortal threats and terror in stupid confusion . . . / Is the fate of a planet still to be decided?" All is compromised by the conflicts of history: "Commotion, power, war, crime." In fine: "a purely human disorder. "Errors with sorrows, / disasters. / Ah, the wars of Cain!" The economic factor is also present: "Even the reddish sunsets are wounded / by terrible rivers / of numbers with zeros, / the zeros of those men." Evil exists within the disorder, and the worldview must be ethical. Demonic symbols stand out. "The dragon has intervened or is it a gargoyle / who vomits, who laughs." They are the executors of negation. "Revolt against being!" Therefore, "Dissonant and grotesque, they deny, they kill." At night one glimpses "Evil with its tortoises, its gargoyles, / night below sinking in the mud, falling." Certainly—and this is the faith that sustains this *Cántico*—evil does not prevail. "Although it increases its tangle, / evil does not sway" in the cosmos.

Pain bears an unfriendly countenance. It is true that not all of its effects are evil. No matter: it always meets with firm resistance. When the "intruder" departs, the sick one exclaims "I am now who I am." Pain undermines and destroys the unity of being. "I am not my illness." Suffering, "I lose myself in disorder." Of course pain and sorrow inform and form one, they elucidate and fortify. There is no life without that component. But the truly normal man never abandons himself to such a negation of being. The coherence of *Cántico* permits no other conduct. "Pain! Resigned and impatient, / he awaits his phase of freedom, / of his vibrant, harmonious power." His relationship with the world is suspended. "Nothing exists / around the afflicted heart." Satisfaction with sorrow or affliction would be morbid. "As much as the arm cavils / no, there is no lament." After the "suffered affliction," comes the containing. "No, no weeping." An ominous wind blows. "But the wind / will not put out my falling lights." To anguish ("Jail from the eyelids to the soul") one brings, as consolation, a non-human light, because "Light, which never suffers, / guides me well." That doesn't prevent one from sharing one's afflictions with others. "Does your grief hide you? It seeks mine." It is the combined war against the adversary. "Pain? Fury of being. Thus we suffer." Even in that conjuncture, the will's vigor is exacerbated. "I don't believe in number 13." "An anguish common / to all . . . ." All the more reason for resisting. "I will not yield, I do not give up."

Fortunate and unfortunate contingencies keep occurring through time. "Of a time proceeding always to its ruin!" At times love predominates: "At the head of bitter living!" The temporal flow tightens and deepens in the present, the time preferred by *Cántico*. Time still flows: "The afternoon / vibrated like those / now past— do you recall? / those intimate and spacious afternoons." The historical past is evoked. "Along illustrious shores" there wanders a Fragrance of cool / centuries!" Love opens toward the future: "I need to feel / that you are beneath my lips, / in today's joy / necessary tomorrow"—a tomorrow which is necessary also to our collective hope. "In the air a free / future . . . ." Love is a "Love of many days," not of special days. "Monday, Tuesday, et cetera, / precious discordant et cetera / also sustenance and continuing reality." Time thus is joined to space as a supporting base: the days are not lost. "What became of those days that passed swiftly / through the heart?" Days remain, in their fashion, in memory, united to certain places. "Time is profundity: it is in gardens." "Here the years are in rhythm with time." It is also, with greater spaciousness, on the ancestral ground. "A great present: tableland / of centuries . . . ." Centuries prodded by hope, one of the sources of *Cántico,* go "Always toward their future, their infinite."

Temporality is mortality. Death appears at the moment of its transpiring—"Tránsito"—or afterward: "The dead are more dead / every night." Another garden: "Vertical stone, / the names of the others." These others are in peace now, with "Skeleton without anguish, solitary bone." Such an emotion only affects the living. "At

17

times I am troubled by a certainty, / and there before me trembles my future." Nevertheless, the trembling is overcome, and death is thought of as an end required by life's very order. The cemetery's white wall "Will impose on me its law, not its accident." We should resign ourselves to die with serenity, and, if possible, "without tears." Our hand touches the head's skull. "It presses the already dead bone." Nevertheless, death does not appear on the horizon as orientation for life. "Death: I live not for you." Life is not a slow dying. "Wait. Just once, / once only! Wait." Mortality is not death.

IV

18   All of these deforming and destructive influences constitute the chorus of *Cántico,* a minor chorus of voices, secondary with respect to the singing voice. Near or remote, they remain in the background, quite capable of figuring as protagonists. Such they will be on other stages, and with such robust accents that they will form a "clamor." [*Clámor* is the name of the book that followed *Cántico*—Translator's note.] Here their existence suffices as a part of the whole. Only thus does it form a complete vision, without mutilations that would alter the truth. "Never, never chosen deceits!" therefore, "More, more truth!" There is no need for an "obscuration / with screens in reserve."

The garden itself, a triumph of selection, is not isolated. It is surrounded by "The discordant world around." The man who enjoys that "serene moment" says to himself "Here you have reality / disturbance: a harsh farrago. / And the garden? Where the garden?

/ —In its midst." The affirmation of reality rises above its confusion and bitterness. When pain retreats, one ascends: "I rushed aloft." The storm—"Purple alarm"— is seen as the eve of the pellucid day to follow. Lovers declare their love in public, and while they commit themselves, "They are not unaware that they rise to a greater / risk, hidden always," the risk of all living things. "Always life by a hairbreadth?" Therefore "Being wars against nothingness," against the opposing chorus. A chorus which acts even in the mist: a minor difficulty, but significant. "Give back to me, mist, give me back what is mine: / the holy things, volume with its dew."

The city offers a contradictory mélange. "Who made it so / terrible, who so beautiful? / The city is indivisible: it is itself." Thus: "The ugly / side by side with the beautiful, over swift clouds, / between the sky and desire." One declares: "O sun-swept joy!" And the other replies: "And the rest, long and grey / between two lights." Or what is the same: "A love well lived . . . But so many sorrows / endured! Love, love—now bitter, now sweet. / Who would not sigh!" This man, "however," never gives in to pusillanimous resignation. Even the "love well lived," now "daily substance," bears with it interludes of aridity and depressions. "Suddenly, a desert crackles beneath the foot / with a sharp-petaled flower . . . ." The soul is destitute if it is alone. "Reality, reality, do not abandon me / the better to dream the deep dream!" that of reality fully accepted.

The outcome sounds like a victory. The lovers evade confusion and outrage: "so much diffuse crime, so many deceiving accomplices."—and they make their way "in spite of everything." The "Eastern Balconies" is an ironic title, a troubled dawn. "Impoverished wine-door / surprised by life!" A tavern is alluded to, and its zinc counter, and a neighborhood with faded signs. In another dawn, that of the son who begins to live, the world is offered as a treasure. "Flames and embers? / The world, invading, creates itself, / an immense world /of truths, / an immense truth / of blood. / Son: / your world, your treasure."

There are never elegant lies. Positive and negative values are not dissociated in that unified vision. *Cántico* insists on this adherence to reality exactly as it is. "Confusion? The distress / of indivisible life. / There is no other. Let it go on, then! / I will plunge into its turmoil." One faces up only to real, to earthly life. "The future will sink into that / pleasant and painful pulp of years. / Sorrow? Yes, also. Fatal? None is excused. / All, all, within! There are no strangers." It is a situation which makes one think of its opposite. "Perfect summer beneath the sun! Peace / ripens. Was there never strife?"

One looks at, one must look at, the world face to face. In the finale to *Cántico*—"Face to Face"—one prepares to meet the invading chorus. It is there, known and surveyed. Then the dangerous band must be made to keep its distance. Man does not surrender so easily to his enemies. *Cántico* champions the struggle for being, the combat against non-being. One does not take the gift of life for granted; rather one exercises, above all, the will to live. "Here am I face to face / with reality. I do not hide, I push on stubbornly. / I do not cede, I will not give in, always in wonder." Since this impetus toward values is so fervent, and since these values are not confined to a specific zone, one must face up to the totality of life. "I need a possible anguish / to limit my joys / that they be held within the most real / day that I encounter. / Thus let reality break / against my shoals and reefs, / let a contradictory / swell surround me, / and let me be found in the center / of truth"—truth the only object.

But it is impossible to compromise with evil. "Insufferable disruption! There is no way out: / to deny negation / and overcome its legions." Having taken this path, one encounters sacrifice. The hero, ready to give his life, is "living at its utmost. He is the greatest yea-sayer." *Cántico* is formed of contemplation and action. Both are directed toward a single end: to intensify the consciousness, the wholeness of our being in the world. "There is no fortune / greater than this concordance / of being with being." Unfortunate is the man who loses this equilibrium. One realizes, then, the existence of this essential harmony that his ear neither hears nor listens to. *Cántico* seeks to pay attention to this immediate, themeless present. What happens then? Nothing but the formidable convergence of Creation. He who glimpses this convergence can sum up his wonder in a few words: "The world is well made." The world is a splendid Creation which in itself contains its failures and excellences. "And all one's being submerges, tranquilly / and vigorously in the peace of the universe, / the vast peace which shelters strife / all immersed in the immense tide." From encircling Creation one has passed to the creative impulse, which proclaims faith in man, in his present and future. The flood tide is a harmonious peak between tide and tide. [Omitted here is a verse (page 466 of *Cántico*) which, based on the onomatopoeic repetition of the word *mar* (sea), is untranslatable.] The swimmer emerges on the shores of the universe and in his human corner. "This world of man is badly made." Not that other world, superior to man. Society and Creation are never confused in *Cántico*; there is not a single phrase devoted to a past or present historical conglomerate.

Of course, no literary page can evade history entirely, but "historical" is not a distinguishing trait. Waking and sleeping, soliloquy and colloquy, comings and goings through fields and cities, love and the pleasures of *Cántico* are individual or social history, but dateless. *Cántico* describes how these things are tied together across the years, these things which, as their general traits are depicted, consolidate the, shall we say, permanently repeated history. *Cántico* attempts to reach this supreme level. The sleeper awakens every day. Such a happening, of greatest importance, is dateless.

The single acts or groups of acts that determine the progress and the aspect of each epoch occupy a visible position: that of dated history. The epoch of *Cántico* is one that can be circumscribed chronologically. "A truck filled with violent men will pass" one afternoon of the Civil War, of "emphatic uproar" of "so many men." After a splendid twilight, in the early evening, a solitary passer-by, troubled and harassed, crosses the "Four Streets." The streets' showy appearance contrasts with their dictatorial actuality. "This excess of brilliance becomes sinister." No doubt that "this world of men is badly made," the world of those terrible years, impelled from "boards of revelry and pride" by a "Cajoling voice that now / suddenly becomes ominous, / irate with the air . . . ." They are "The farces, the outrages, / the politics, the damp / snout of a cynically hirsute / animal . . . ." There are wars, with their atrocious camps—"That anguish of a mist / filled only with objects"—and its foul uniformity: "Crime has become law, and all obey." That is our public and dated history. "But the brutal hubbub, / the mob that inundates . . . ," thus begins "Estación del norte." It is the circumstantial "but" added to the essential *Cántico,* to its continual course of recorded dateless days. Besides, each work contributes to the definition of an epoch, and blends into its tone or tones. 1919 to 1950: times and places belonging to a Western and Christian world. (The poems "Christmas" and "Holy Saturday" are as anchors in that tradition.)

"With what glad accord / I consent to my living, / with what childlike fidelity, humbly assenting / I sense my being . . . ." Each morning the "world begins / with all its flowing sources." There is no apotheosis. "The blue rosemary / smacks of true world." Let that small flower be emblematic, because "The truth charms dawns."

Cántico is an act of attention. "What full / measure awaits the step of the attentive!" The attentive one proposes an "exercise in shared wholeness," in friendship and love. Among contrarities one tends toward serenity, toward a joy accompanied by wondrous gratitude. "This ground? Tableland on which I am struck by / so much unmerited reality, / occasion for my joy," and this is not precisely a private happiness, caused by individual motives. Gladness! "I sense it so intimately, so virile and real / that it becomes one with my essence." The reasons? Well—"Just because, because it is my fate, / I am strongly partial to the universe," that is prodigious "besides." The experience of being, the affirmation of life, of this terrestrial life, valuable in itself, and for the present, a canticle. And the canticle resolves itself into a form whose sound and sense are inseparable. Thought and feeling, image and cadence, establish a unity, and only in that unity can exist that which is sought: poetry.

(Returning to flesh, the soul
veers toward the eyes
and strikes.) Light! It floods
all my being. Wonder! . . .

Part I: from *Cántico*

de Más allá

(El alma vuelve al cuerpo,
Se dirige a los ojos
Y choca.) —¡Luz! Me invade
Todo mi ser. ¡Asombro!

Intacto aún, enorme,
Rodea el tiempo . . . Ruidos
Irrumpen. ¡Cómo saltan
Sobre los amarillos

26

Todavía no agudos
De un sol hecho ternura
De rayo alboreado
Para estancia difusa,

Mientras van presentándose
Todas las consistencias
Que al disponerse en cosas
Me limitan, me centran!

¿Hubo un caos? Muy lejos
De su origen, me brinda
Por entre hervor de luz
Frescura en chispas. ¡Día!

Una seguridad
Se extiende, cunde, manda.

from Beyond

(Returning to flesh, the soul
veers toward the eyes
and strikes.) Light! It floods
my being. Wonder! Whole,

immense, Time surrounds
me . . . Noises break forth.
How they leap over the
still unsharp, the rounded

yellows, the fragile amber
of the sun's dawning, soft
rays that suffuse this wide
awakening chamber,

while there gradually
take shape consistencies
which, on becoming things,
limit and center me!

Was there a chaos? Drawn
from its source, it offers
me in a surge of gleaming
coolness: the day, the dawn.

A certainty is born,
it deepens, commands.

El esplendor aploma
La insinuada mañana.

Y la mañana pesa,
Vibra sobre mis ojos,
Que volverán a ver
Lo extraordinario: todo.

Todo está concentrado
Por siglos de raíz
Dentro de este minuto,
Eterno y para mí.

Y sobre los instantes
Que pasan de continuo
Voy salvando el presente,
Eternidad en vilo.

Corre la sangre, corre
Con fatal avidez.
A ciegas acumulo
Destino: quiero ser.

Ser, nada más. Y basta.
Es la absoluta dicha.
¡Con la esencia en silencio
Tanto se identifica!

¡Al azar de las suertes
Únicas de un tropel

The splendor consummates
the suggested morn.

And the morning falls,
vibrates on my eyes
that will behold again
the marvelous: all.

All is entwined
through rooted centuries
within this moment:
eternal and mine.

Over the endless, spare,
hurrying instants,
I save the present,
eternity in air.

The blood runs, runs free,
with fatal avidity.
Blindly I assemble
destiny: I want to be.

And nothing more: to be.
It is enough. Its joy is
absolute. It conforms
with essence silently.

By chance from fleeing
lots, helter-skelter chosen,

Surgir entre los siglos,
Alzarse con el ser,

Y a la fuerza hundirse
Con la sonoridad
Más tenaz: sí, sí, sí,
La palabra del mar!

Todo me comunica,
Vencedor, hecho mundo,
Su brío para ser
De veras real, en triunfo.

30

Soy, más, estoy. Respiro.
Lo profundo es el aire.
La realidad me inventa,
Soy su leyenda. ¡Salve!

to surge up in centuries,
to carry off Being,

and perforce to blend
with the most tenacious
sonority: yes, yes, yes,
the word the sea lends

us. Everything yields
to me—victor, made world—
its determination
to be triumphantly real.

I am; I am here and now.
I breathe the deepest air.
Reality invents me.
I am its legend. Hail!

Los nombres

Albor. El horizonte
Entreabre sus pestañas
Y empieza a ver. ¿Qué? Nombres.
Están sobre la pátina

De las cosas. La rosa
Se llama todavía
Hoy rosa, y la memoria
De su tránsito, prisa,

Prisa de vivir más.
¡A largo amor nos alce
Esa pujanza agraz
Del Instante, tan ágil

Que en llegando a su meta
Corre a imponer Después!
¡Alerta, alerta, alerta,
Yo seré, yo seré!

¿Y las rosas? Pestañas
Cerradas: horizonte
Final. ¿Acaso nada?
Pero quedan los nombres.

The Names

Dawn. The horizon
opens its lashes,
begins to see. What? Names.
They are on the patina

of things. The rose
is still called
rose, and the memory
of its passing, haste.

Haste to live more, more!
May the instant's acrid
plunge lift us, move
us to unending love! So

swift in reaching its
goal it rushes to impose
later! Watch out, I shall
be! And the roses?

Closed eyelids, final
horizon. And there remains
nothing, at all? No,
there are still the names.

El manantial

Mirad bien. ¡Ahora!
Blancuras en curva
Triunfalmente una
—Frescor hacia forma—

Guían su equilibrio
Por entre el tumulto
—Pródigo, futuro—
De un caos ya vivo.

El agua desnuda
Se desnuda más.
¡Más, más, más! Carnal,
Se ahonda, se apura.

¡Más, más! Por fin . . . ¡Viva!
Manantial, doncella:
Escorzo de piernas,
Tornasol de guijas.

Y emerge—compacta
Del río que pudo
Ser, esbelto y curvo—
Toda la muchacha.

The Source

Now then: behold!
Whiteness in curves
triumphantly one
—form-seeking cold—

guides its symmetry
among a tumult
—prodigiously future—
of a living flurry.

The naked flow
sheds its garments.
More, more! Carnal,
it deepens, it grows.

More! At last . . . Hurray!
The spring, the maiden:
a vision of limbs,
pebbles' bright spray.

At last, in a swirl,
emerges—from the river
that could be, slender and
curved—superbly, the girl.

Naturaleza viva

¡Tablero de la mesa
Que, tan exactamente
Raso nivel, mantiene
Resuelto en una idea

Su plano: puro, sabio,
Mental para los ojos
Mentales! Un aplomo,
Mientras, requiere al tacto,

Que palpa y reconoce
Cómo el plano gravita
Con pesadumbre rica
De leña, tronco, bosque

De nogal. ¡El nogal
Confiado a sus nudos
Y vetas, a su mucho
Tiempo de potestad

Reconcentrada en este
Vigor inmóvil, hecho
Materia de tablero
Siempre, siempre silvestre!

Unstill Life

Surface of a table
which, so nicely, smoothly
level, fixes its levelness

in an idea: pure, wise,
mental for mental eyes!
Certainty, meanwhile,
depends on touch

which presses, discovers
how the surface weighs
with its rich heaviness
of wood, trunk, walnut

forest. The walnut confides
in its knots and grain,
in its long span of power,

concentrated in this
motionless vigor, become
this tabletop, surface,
forever the forest.

Impaciente vivir

Salta por el asfalto,
Frente al anochecer,
El ventarrón de marzo,
Tan duro que se ve.

Las esquinas aguzan
Su coraje incisivo.
Tiemblan desgarraduras
De viento y sol. ¿Gemidos?

Una lid: cuatro calles.
La luz bamboleada,
Luz apenas, retrae
Las figuras a manchas.

Da el viento anochecido
Contra esquina y sillar.
Marzo arrecia. ¿Granito?
Él lo acometerá.

Entonces, por la piedra
Rebotando, se yergue
Con más gana la fuerza
Del vivir impaciente.

Impatient Life

It leaps on the asphalt
confronting the evening,
the bully March wind:
so strong, it is seen.

The quick corners sharpen
its incisive anger.
There tremble tatters
of wind and sun. Laments?

A struggle: four streets.
The reeling light toils.
Dying, it withdraws
its figures by strokes.

Dark now, the wind rams
against corner and slab.
March digs in. Granite?
The wind will assail it.

Then, rebounding off stone,
with vigorous stride,
the force of impatient
life swells, swells with pride.

Advenimiento

¡Oh luna, cuánto abril,
Qué vasto y dulce el aire!
Todo lo que perdí
Volverá con las aves.

Sí, con las avecillas
Que en coro de alborada
Pían y pían, pían
Sin designio de gracia.

La luna está muy cerca,
Quieta en el aire nuestro.
El que yo fui me espera
Bajo mis pensamientos.

Cantará el ruiseñor
En la cima del ansia.
Arrebol, arrebol
Entre el cielo y las auras.

¿Y se perdió aquel tiempo
Que yo perdí? La mano
Dispone, dios ligero,
De esta luna sin año.

Advent

Oh moon, what presence of April!
How vast and sweet the air!
All that I lost
the songbirds restore.

Yes, the small birds
that in sunrise glee
sing and chirp
artlessly.

Quiet in this air,
the moon is near.
That which I was
awaits me here.

The nightingale will sing
at the height of desire.
Between the air and sky,
clouds incarnadine.

Those years, are they doomed
to oblivion? The hand
disposes, fickle god,
of this timeless moon.

Sabor a vida

Hay ya cielo por el aire
Que se respira.
Respiro, floto en venturas,
Por alegrías.

Las alegrías de un hombre
Se ahondan fuera esparcidas.
Yo soy feliz en los árboles,
En el calor, en la umbría.

¿Aventuras? No las caza
Mi cacería.
Tengo con el mismo sol
La eterna cita.

¡Actualidad! Tan fugaz
En su cogollo y su miga,
Regala a mi lentitud
El sumo sabor a vida.

¡Lenta el alma, lentos pasos
En compañía!
¡La gloria posible nunca,
Nunca abolida!

Lifetaste

There's a sky now in the deeply
      savored air,
I breathe, I drift through joys
      haphazardly.

The joys of a man
deepen, invade.
I am content with the trees,
in the heat, in the shade.

Adventures? My hunting dogs
      hound them not.
I have with the sun itself
      a meeting spot.

The present!—so elusive
in its marrow and pith,
regales my loitering
with the utmost taste of life.

Slow the soul, slow footsteps
      accompanied!
Oh possible glory never,
      never denied!

Descanso en jardín

Los astros avanzan entre
    Nubarrones
Hacia el último jardín.
        Losas, flores.

¿Qué del incidente humano?
        Calma en bloque.
Los muertos están más muertos
        Cada noche.

Mármoles, frondas iguales:
        Verde el orden.
Sobre el ciprés unos astros:
        Más verdores.

Muriendo siguen los muertos.
        ¡Bien se esconden
Entre la paz y el olvido,
        Sin sus nombres!

Haya para el gran cansancio
        Sombra acorde.
Los astros se acercan entre
        Nubarrones.

Calm of Gardens

The stars advance among
    storm clouds
toward the final garden.
    Stones, flowers.

What of the human accident?
    Block-like quiet.
The dead are more dead
    every night.

Marbles, fronds all alike:
    green is the order.
Over the cypress, stars:
    more verdure.

The dead go on dying.
    Well they remain
in peace and oblivion
    bereft of their names!

May their weariness enjoy
    shade in accord.
The stars approach among
    storm clouds.

Cima de la delicia

¡Cima de la delicia!
Todo en el aire es pájaro.
Se cierne lo inmediato
Resuelto en lejanía.

¡Hueste de esbeltas fuerzas!
¡Qué alacridad de mozo
En el espacio airoso,
Henchido de presencia!

El mundo tiene cándida
Profundidad de espejo.
Las más claras distancias
Sueñan lo verdadero.

¡Dulzura de los años
Irreparables! ¡Bodas
Tardías con la historia
Que desamé a diario!

Más, todavía más.
Hacia el sol, en volandas
La plenitud se escapa.
¡Ya sólo sé cantar!

Summit of Delight

Summit of delight!
All the air is bird.
The moment takes flight,
resolves into distance.

Host of slender forces!
What a surge of youth
in the buoyant space
filled with presence!

The world has the lucid
depth of a mirror.
The clearest distances
dream the true.

Charm of irreparable
years! Yes, late
marriage with that history
I scorned day by day.

More, still more.
Toward the sun on wings
plenitude escapes.
Now can I only sing!

Vida urbana

Calles, un jardín,
Césped—y sus muertos.
Morir, no, vivir.
¡Qué urbano lo eterno!

Losa vertical,
Nombres de los otros.
La inmortalidad
Preserva su otoño.

¿Y aquella aflicción?
Nada sabe el césped
De ningún adiós.
¿Dónde está le muerte?

Hervor de la ciudad
En torno a las tumbas.
Una misma paz
Se cierne difusa.

Juntos, a través
Ya de un solo olvido,
Quedan en tropel
Los muertos, los vivos.

Urban Living

Streets, a garden,
grass—and its dead.
To die, no, to live.
How urban the eternal!

Vertical stone,
names of the others.
Immortality
preserves its autumn.

And that affliction?
The grass knows nothing
of any goodbye.
Where then is death?

A city's agitation
around the graves.
An accustomed peace
hovers diffused.

Together immersed
in forgetfulness,
in a noisy jumble,
the living, the dead.

Primavera delgada

Cuando el espacio sin perfil resume
    Con una nube
Su vasta indecisión a la deriva,
    —¿Dónde la orilla?—
Mientras el río con el rumbo en curva
    Se perpetúa
Buscando sesgo a sesgo, dibujante,
    Su desenlace,
Mientras el agua duramente verde
    Niega sus peces
Bajo el profundo equívoco reflejo
    De un aire trémulo . . .
Cuando conduce la mañana, lentas,
    Sus alamedas
Gracias a las estelas vibradoras
    Entre las frondas,
A favor del avance sinuoso
    Que pone en coro
La ondulación suavísima del cielo
    Sobre su viento
Con el curso tan ágil de las pompas,
    Que agudas bogan . . .
¡Primavera delgada entre los remos
    De los barqueros!

Slender Spring

When space without profile resumes
    in a cloud
its vast indecision set adrift
    (where the shore?)
while the river with its curved route
    repeats itself
seeking, line by line (gentle artist)
    its conclusion,
while the opaquely green water
    denies its fish
beneath the deep equivocal reflection
    of a tremulous air . . .
When the morning conducts, slowly,
    its poplar groves
thanks to the vibrating wake
    between the fronds,
assisted by the winding progress
    that puts in tune
the soft undulation of the sky
    over its wind
with the agile course of the bubbles
    that intently row . . .
Slender Spring between the oars
    of the boatmen!

Desnudo

Blancos, rosas. Azules casi en veta,
Retraídos, mentales.
Puntos de luz latente dan señales
De una sombra secreta.

Pero el color, infiel a la penumbra,
Se consolida en masa.
Yacente en el verano de la casa,
Una forma se alumbra.

Claridad aguzada entre perfiles,
De tan puros tranquilos,
Que cortan y aniquilan con sus filos
Las confusiones viles.

Desnuda está la carne. Su evidencia
Se resuelve en reposo.
Monotonía justa, prodigioso
Colmo de la presencia.

¡Plenitud inmediata, sin ambiente,
Del cuerpo femenino!
Ningún primor: ni voz ni flor. ¿Destino?
¡Oh absoluto Presente!

Nude

Whites. Pinks. Blues in veins, mental,
      grow and fade.
Points of latent light show signs
      or a secret shade.

But color, false to the penumbra,
      in mass resurges.
Supine in the summer of the house,
      a form emerges.

Clarity sharpened by profiles,
      so tranquil and pure,
they cut, destroy with their edges
      the base confusions.

Naked is the flesh. Its evidence
      resolves in repose.
The right monotone, prodigious
      measure of presence.

Stark fullness, without ambience,
      of the female form!
No gloss: voice nor flower. Destiny?
      Oh Present unadorned!

Noche de luna

Altitud veladora:
Descienden ya vigías
Por tanta luz de luna.

¡Astral candor del mar!
Los plumajes del frío
Tensamente se ciernen.

Y, planicie, la espera:
Callada se difunde
La expectación de espuma.

54

¡Ah! ¿Por fin? Desde el fondo
Los sueños de las algas
A la noche iluminan.

Voluntad de lo leve:
Adorables arenas
Exigen gracia al viento.

¡Ascensión a lo blanco!
Los muertos más profundos,
Aire en el aire, van.

Difícil delgadez:
¿Busca el mundo una blanca,
Total, perenne ausencia?

Moonlit Night

Guardian height:
vigils descend
through so much moonlight.

Astral candor of the sea!
The plumages of cold
tensely soar free.

Plateau-like abiding,
Quietly is diffused
the expectation of foam.

55

Ah! Finally? From the depth
the dreams of the algae
illuminate the night.

Will of the lambent:
adorable sands
demand grace of the wind.

Ascension to white!
The most profound dead
stir, air in the air.

Difficult lightness:
does the world seek a white,
total, perennial absence?

Estatua ecuestre

Permanece el trote aquí

Entre su arranque y mi mano.

Bien ceñida queda así

Su intención de ser lejano.

Porque voy en un corcel

A la maravilla fiel:

Inmóvil con todo brío.

¡Y a la fuerza de cuánta calma

Tengo en bronce toda el alma,

Clara en el cielo del frío!

Equestrian Statue

The horse's gallop remains
between my hand and its start.
Its ambition to be far
is thus firmly restrained.
Because I ride a steed
that's marvelously true:
motionless with all its might.
By dint of so much calm
my soul is charged with bronze
clear in the winter light!

57

El arco de medio punto

Muro a muro, hueco a hueco,
La Historia es este descanso
Donde opera aún el eco
De una gran voz, hoy ya manso
Discurrir de una armonía
Presente. Le galería
Conduce hasta el gran conjunto,
Que muda todo sol en luz
Serena. ¡Mira bien
El arco de medio punto!

58

The Roman Arch

Wall after wall, hollow to hollow,
history is this rare repose
where there yet exists the echo
of a great voice, now the muffled
discourse of a harmony sounded
still. As curve on curve rebounds
the tranquil colonnade compels
the sight to a splendid oneness
that mutes all suns in serene light.
The rounded Roman arch: look well.

59

Beato sillón

¡Beato sillón! La casa
Corrobora su presencia
Con la vaga intermitencia
De su invocación en masa
A la memoria. No pasa
Nada. Los ojos no ven,
Saben. El mundo está bien
Hecho. El instante lo exalta
A marea, de tan alta,
De tan alta, sin vaivén.

Blessed Armchair

Blessed armchair! The house
corroborates its presence
with the vague intermittence
of its invocation *en masse*
to the memory. Nothing
happens. The eyes do not see,
they know. The world is well
made. The instant exalts it
to flood tide, to a certain
plenitude, unwavering.

61

Perfección

Queda curvo el firmamento,

Compacto azul, sobre el día.

Es el redondeamiento

Del esplendor: mediodía.

Todo es cúpula. Reposa,

Central sin querer, la rosa,

A un sol en cenit sujeta.

Y tanto se da el presente

Que el pie caminante siente

La integridad del planeta.

Perfection

The firmament is curved,
compact blue, over the day.
Splendor's roundness: noon.
All being is cupola.
The rose, indifferent
center, rests, subject
to the sun. And the Present
gives of itself so freely
that the treading foot senses
the planet's integrity.

Vaso de agua

No es mi sed, no son mis labios

Quienes se placen en esa

Frescura, ni con resabios

De museo se embelesa

Mi visión de tal aplomo:

Líquido volumen como

Cristal que fuese aun más terso.

Vista y fe son a la vez

Quienes te ven, sencillez

Última del universo.

Glass of Water

It's not my lips, not my thirst
that derive unswerving pleasure
from this coolness; nor the measure
of my sight (museum's aftertaste)
charmed by such tranquility:
liquid of a greater constancy
than glass. Not my lips and thirst
but sight and faith together
joined observe you, ultimate
refinement of the universe.

Muerte a lo lejos

Je soutenais l'éclat de la mort
toute pure.—Paul Valéry

Alguna vez me angustia una certeza,
Y ante mí se estremece mi futuro.
Acechándole está de pronto un muro
Del arrabal final en que tropieza

La luz del campo. ¿Más habrá tristeza
Si la desnuda el sol? No, no hay apuro
Todavía. Lo urgente es el maduro
Fruto. La mano ya le descorteza.

... Y un día entre los días el más triste
Será. Tenderse deberá la mano
Sin afán. Y acatando el inminente

Poder diré sin lágrimas: embiste,
Justa fatalidad. El muro cano
Va a imponerme su ley, no su accidente.

66

Death in the Distance

*Je soutenais l'éclat de la mort
toute pure.*—PAUL VALÉRY

At times I am troubled by a certainty
and there before me trembles my future.
In its sudden ambush looms a wall
of the final suburb on which is cast

the field's light. But shall there be grief
if the sun bares it? No, there is no anguish
yet. More urgent is the full ripe
fruit that the hand already peels.

... And that will be the most sad among
days. Then let the hand offer and fall
without despair. And revering the imminent

Power I shall say without tears: come,
just fatality. The white wall
will impose on me its law, not its accident.

Preferida a Venus

De las ondas
Terminante perfil entre espumas sin forma,

Imprevista
Surge—lejos su patria—la seducción marina.

¡Salve, tú
Que de la tierra vienes para ser en lo azul

No deidad
Soñada sino cuerpo de prodigio real!

Nadadora
Feliz va regalando desnudez a las ondas.

Preferred to Venus

From the tide,
precise profile in formless foam,

suddenly
surges—far her homeland—sea-borne seduction.

Hail to you
land-born voyager to become in the blue

not imagined
goddess, but female form, potently real!

The swimmer
happily regales her nakedness to the waves.

Esos cerros

¿Pureza, soledad? Allí. Son grises.

Grises intactos que ni el pie perdido

Sorprendió, soberanamente leves.

Grises junto a la Nada melancólica,

Bella, que el aire acoge como un alma,

Visible de tan fiel a un fin: la espera.

¡Ser, ser, y aun más remota, para el humo,

Para los ojos de los más absortos,

Una Nada amparada: gris intacto

Sobre tierna aridez, gris de esos cerros!

The Hills

Purity, solitude? There. They are grey.
Intact greys not even the idle foot
surprised, supremely light. Greys beside
Nothing, melancholy and beautiful, which
the air shelters like a soul, visible
because so true to its object: waiting
always. To be! And even more remote,
for smoke, for eyes of the most distracted,
a secure Nothingness: the perfect grey
on tender aridness, grey of those hills!

Los jardines

Tiempo en profundidad: está en jardines.

Mira cómo se posa. Ya se ahonda.

Ya es tuyo su interior. ¡Qué trasparencia

De muchas tardes, para siempre juntas!

Sí, tu niñez, ya fábula de fuentes.

The Gardens

Time in profundity: it is in gardens.

See how it alights. Then it deepens.

Now its center is yours. What transparence

of many afternoons, forever joined!

Yes, your childhood: now fable of fountains.

Noche encendida

Tiempo: ¿prefieres la noche encendida?

. . . Bien, radiador, ruiseñor del invierno.

¡Qué lentitud, soledad, en tu colmo!

¿La claridad de la lámpara es breve?

Cerré las puertas. El mundo me ciñe.

74

Illuminated Night

Time: do you prefer the night illuminated?

... Well, radiator, winter's nightingale.

Solitude, how leisurely your fullness!

Is the lamp's clarity brief? I closed

the doors. The world embraces me.

75

Más vida

¿Por qué tú, por qué yo bajo el cielo admirable?
¿Por qué azar, por qué turno
De favor, por qué enlace
De laberinto, por qué gracia
De viaje
Prorrumpimos a ser, acertamos a estar
En el instante
Que se arroja hacia la maravilla?

Sí, salve.

II

Hijo, resplandor
De mi júbilo
Como el verso posible
Que busco.

Gracias a ti, figura de mi amor bajo el sol,
Restituído
Todo a esa luz y con alma visible a ti acudo,
Límpido.

En su interior el alma profundiza
Sin oscurecimiento.
Heme aquí de mi noche liberado,
Neto.

More Life

Why you and I beneath the admirable sky?
By what accident, by what
stroke of fate, by what chance
meeting in the
labyrinth
did we burst into being,
did we hit on
this instant
that hurtles toward the marvelous?

Yes: hail.

Son, radiance
of my joy
like the possible verse
I seek.

Thanks to you, image of my love beneath the sun,
restored
to the light
and with my soul visible I come to you.
Transparent.

Inwardly the soul deepens
without darkness.
Behold me free of my night,
without stain.

Hijo, ya impulso hacia la luz
Desde mi gozo:
Hay luz universal
Para tus ojos.

III

¡Cuántos siglos ahora sosteniéndote,
Y con su esfuerzo
Latentes, montañosos,
A tus pies emergiendo
Para levantar un futuro
Todavía tan leve y tan inquieto
Que apenas
Se insinúa en el aire de tu pecho!

IV

La mirada mía verá
Con tus ojos
El mejor universo:
El de tu asombro.

A través de tus horas, sin descanso
Más allá de la muerte,
Hasta el año 2000 he de llegar
Calladamente.

Hijo tan asombrado, tan interior al círculo
del enigma:

Son, impulse toward light
from within my joy:
here is a diffuse splendor
for your sight.

III

How many centuries sustain you
and with their strength
—latent, mountainous—
emerging at your feet
to create a future,
still so airy and restless
hardly
hinted at by your starting breath!

79

IV

My sight will see
with your eyes
the finest universe:
that of your surprise.

Across your hours
without repose
I will touch the next century
quietly.

My son, so deeply
within the circle
of the wondrous
enigma:

La Creación en creación
Es quien te sitia.

v

Hacia su plenitud
Mi mejor pensamiento,
Frente a mí se me planta,
Carne y hueso.
Eres.
      Y yo no soy libre.
¡Que dulce así, ya prisionero
De mi vida más mía,
Ser responsable de tu aliento!
Tu realidad no deja escapatoria.
Eres mi término,
El término fatal de mi ternura.
¡Qué gozo en este apego
Sin ninguna razón,
En este celo
Tan obstinado tras la pequeñez!
Profundo amor pequeño
Me fuerza
—Dentro de un orbe que es un cerco—
A gravitar, y así con mi vivir
Gravito, quiero
Astro dichoso.
¡Oh dicha: preso!
           Preso.

Creation creating
surrounds you.

v

Toward its plenitude
my finest thought
made flesh and blood
stands before me.
You are.
　　　And I am not free.
How agreeable thus
to be prisoner
of my own flesh,
responsible
for your breath!
Your reality leaves no escape.
You are the fatal
finality of my tenderness.
What delight
in this reasonless
attachment,
in this obstinate zeal
toward smallness.
This deep and small love
draws me
—within this circular world—
draws me to itself
and I, happy planet,
yield.
The pleasure of restraint:
　　　　　　　　your prisoner.

¿Quién eres, quién serás?
Existes. Eres. En tu mundo quedo.

VI

Hasta las raíces de mi orgullo profundiza,
Me cala,
Alto y ligero sobre el orgullo levantándome,
Tu gracia.

A tu gracia me rindo
Con mi poder.
Nada se puede contra el ángel.
El ángel es.

Entre las cosas y los sueños
Avanzas
Tan soñado, tan real que me descubro
Más cerca el alma.

VII

Y tú,
Ya con el viento.
¡Qué desgarrón de claridad
En el silencio,
Cuánto espacio de luz esperanzada
En ese acecho
Que es el aire por Junio,
A la gracia dispuesto!

Who are you, what life
will you attain?
You exist. You are. In your
world I remain.

VI

Your charm
goes through to the roots of my pride,
it raises me, high and swift,
above it.

I surrender to it,
I and my power.
You can't beat the *ángel,*
your charm that is.

You proceed among dreams and real things
so dreamlike and real
that I discover
my soul beside me.

VII

And you,
now you and the wind.
What an outburst of clarity
in the silence,
what space of hope-filled light
in that ambush
that is the air in June,
ready for the touch of grace!
And you,
now you and the wind.

Hijo, vislumbre
De gloria:
Cielos redondos ceñirán
Tus obras.

Cima apuntada hacia el azul escueto,
Sin celaje:
El amor mismo te dará
Sus valles.

No soy mi fin, no soy final
De vida.
Pase la corriente. No es tuya
Ni mía.

Hijo, centella
De un fuego:
En el gran fuego inextinguible
Quemémonos.

IX

Ardiendo pasa la corriente. ¡Salve!
Fuegos de creación
Siempre en nosotros, con nosotros arden.

¿Llamas ocultas, de repente en alto,
Brincan, embisten, ágiles?

Errores con dolores,
Desastres.
¡Ay, luchas de Caín!

Son, glimpse
of splendor:
rounded skies will surround
your works.

A sharpened peak toward the thin blueness
no sign of clouds:
love itself will give you
its valleys.

I am not my end, not the finality
of my life.
Let the current flow. It's neither yours
nor mine.

Son, spark
of a fire:
let us burn in the blaze
without end.

IX

The burning flow passes. *Salve!*
Fires of creation
burn in us, burn with us.

Do hidden flames suddenly soar,
leap on-rushing?

Errors with sorrows.
Disasters.
The wars of Cain!

85

Y todo se deshace y se rehace.
¿Llamas y brasas?
Es el mundo invasor y de veras creándose,
Un mundo inmenso
De verdades,
Una inmensa verdad
De sangre.

Hijo:
Tu mundo, tu tesoro.

86

All is undone, all is reborn.
Flames and embers?
The world, invading, creates itself,
an immense world
of truths,
an immense truth
of blood.

Son:
your world, your treasure.

Las doce en el reloj

Dije: ¡Todo ya pleno!
Un álamo vibró.
Las hojas plateadas
Sonaron con amor.
Los verdes eran grises,
El amor era sol.
Entonces, mediodía,
Un pájaro sumió
Su cantar en el viento
Con tal adoración
Que se sintió cantada
Bajo el viento la flor
Crecida entre las mieses,
Más altas. Era yo,
Centro en aquel instante
De tanto alrededor,
Quien lo veía todo
Completo para un dios.
Dije: Todo, completo.
¡Las doce en el reloj!

Twelve O'Clock, Noon

I said: all complete!
A poplar trembled.
Its silvered leaves
rustled lovingly.
Its greens were greying,
its love was the sun.
Then, at midday,
a bird released
its song to the wind
with such adoration
that even a flower
beneath the wind
in the tall grain
heard its praises sung.
It was I, center
at that moment, of
so much existence,
I, who saw all things
replete for a god.
I said: all is perfect.
Twelve o'clock noon.

Salida

¡Salir por fin, salir
A glorias, a rocíos,
—Certera ya la espera,
Ya fatales los ímpetus—
Resbalar sobre el fresco
Dorado del estío
—¡Gracias!—hasta oponer
A las ondas el tino
Gozoso de los músculos
Súbitos del instinto,
Lanzar, lanzar sin miedo
Los lujos y los gritos
A través de la aurora
Central de un paraíso,
Ahogarse en plenitud
Y renacer clarísimo,
—Rachas de espacios vírgenes,
Acordes inauditos—
Feliz, veloz, astral,
Ligero y sin amigo!

The Sally

To set out at last to glory,
to gusts of sea-spray,
(certain the expectation,
fatal the impetus)
to glide over the fresh
gold of summer
(Thanks!) and oppose
to the waves the joyous
skill of the sudden
muscles of instinct,
to fling fearlessly
pleasures and cries
across the central
dawn of a paradise,
to drown in plenitude
and be reborn most clearly,
(blasts of virgin space,
unheard-of chords)
happy, swift, astral,
light and alone!

Callejeo

No sabe adónde va.

Ni le orienta la nube

Próxima que en el cielo

Se aísla, ni conduce

Por sí mismo sus pasos.

Le impulsa la costumbre

De pisar y avanzar.

Nada tal vez más dulce

Ni de mayor consuelo

Que la tarde de un lunes

Cualquiera paseado

De pronto. No trascurre

La hora. Permanece

Con todo su volumen

Bajo la mano aquel

Tiempo sin norte, dúctil,

Propicio a revelar

Algo impar en el cruce

De unas calles. ¡Perderse,

Hacerse muchedumbre!

Callejeo

He knows not where he goes.
Nor does the nearby cloud,
alone in the sky, show him
the way; his very steps are not
his own, compelled by custom
of walking, advancing.
No greater consolation,
perhaps, than an aimless
unexpected Monday
afternoon spent walking.
Time doesn't pass. It remains
with all its fullness beneath
his hand, that random Time,
docile, ready to reveal
something peregrine at the
next street crossing. To lose
oneself, to become the crowd!

Part II: from *Clamor*

Todos o casi todos los hombres

Mientras muchos nos amenazan
Y otros nos muerden,
Los hay que en sus cálculos cuentan
Con . . . nuestra muerte.

¡Qué puras así nuestras vidas,
Siempre al servicio
De una mortandad planeada
Con lápiz fino!

Oíd, directores del mundo:
Agradecemos
—Rehusando—todo ese amor
A grito en cuello.

¿No nacimos para llenar
Nuestro vivir
Y responder a su demanda
Con un gran Sí?

Dejad que nuestra sangre corra
Donde se mueve,
Dejad que sea nuestra vida
Más que su muerte.

All men, or Almost

While many threaten
    and others oppress
there are those who count
    on ... our death.

How pure our lives are,
    ever at the command
of a massacre reckoned
    with a fine hand!

Hear, O world's directors:
    We gratefully decline
so much love offered
    with a chilling whine.

Weren't we born to comply
    with life's promise
and to answer its query
    with a loud Yes?

Let our blood flow
    where it will,
let our life be
    more than our death.

Dafne a medias

UN MISERABLE NÁUFRAGO

Se aleja el Continente con bruma hacia más brumas,
Y es ya rincón y ruina, derrumbe repetido,
Rumores de cadenas chirriando entre lodos.
Adiós, adiós, Europa, te me vas de mi alma,
De mi cuerpo cansado, de mi chaqueta vieja.
El vapor se fué a pique bajo un mar implacable.
A la vez que las ratas huí de la derrota.
Entre las maravillas del pretérito ilustre
Perdéis ese futuro sin vosotros futuro,
Gentes de tanta Historia que ya se os escapa
De vuestras manos torpes, ateridas, inútiles.
Yo no quiero anularme soñando en un vacío
Que llenen las nostalgias. Ay, sálvese el que pueda
Contra el destino. Gracias, orilla salvadora
Que me acoges, me secas, me vistes y me nutres.
En hombros me levantas, nuevo mundo inocente,
Para dejarme arriba. Y si tuya es la cúspide,
Con tu gloria de estío quisiera confundirme,
Y sin pasado exánime participar del bosque,
Ser tronco y rama y flor de un laurel arraigado.
América, mi savia: ¿nunca llegaré a ser?
Apresúrame, please, esta metamorfosis.
Mis cabellos se mueven con susurros de hojas.
Mi brazo vegetal concluye en mano humana.

Half-way Daphne

A WRETCHED CASTAWAY

The continent recedes mistbound toward greater
mist, now desolation and repeated doom,
chains clashing in the deepening mud.
Farewell, O Europe, take your feckless leave
of my soul, my weary body, my threadbare coat.
Like the rats I fled the holocaust,
the ship overwhelmed beneath inexorable seas.
Among the marvels of a splendid past
you let the future slip between your fingers;
burdened with history, that History eludes
your clumsy, shivering, bungling hands. I would
not perish dreaming in a void fertile
with stale nostalgias. Every man for himself
against destiny! Thanks, succoring shore
that receives, dries, clothes and nourishes me.
Lift me on your shoulders, innocent
New World, far from harm. And if yours is
the flood tide, I would join your vernal glory,
shedding my dead past, become a tree
in your forest, trunk and branch and flower
of deep-rooted laurel. America, my sustenance:
hasten your alchemy, quicken, please, this
metamorphosis. My hair rustles with leaves,
my plant-like arm concludes in human hand.

Muy Señor mío

Escribo para ser el blanco
De tus ojos y de tus lentes.
Pero no temas—¡oh, lector,
Ah, posible!—que yo te estreche
Con ruegos, anuncios, visitas
Y lecturas, erre que erre.
Nuestra relación—voluntaria,
Si surge—no sabe de leyes.
El que quiera picar, que pique,
Y el que no quiera, que lo deje.

My Dear Sir

I write to be the object
of your glasses and your eyes.
But do not, therefore, surmise
I will hound you—O potential
reader!—with appeals, subject
you to visits and torrential
readings, day after day.
Our voluntary relation
will admit no legislation.
If you would lend an ear, then stay.
If you don't care to: on your way.

Nada importaría nada

—¡Grande el saber! Nuestro exceso

Va alzando tal espesura

Que inmensamente insegura

Gira la Tierra. —¡Confieso

Que no nací para eso!

Tan docta es ya la jugada

Que al indocto no le agrada.

—Total si en un cataclismo

Pereciese el astro mismo,

¿Importaría? —No, nada.

Not at All

—Great is knowledge! Our excess
has attained to such a girth
that limpingly the earth
spins on its axis. —I confess
I was hardly born for this.
So learned is the diversion
that the unlearned are appalled.
—Well, and if in a final flourish
the orb itself should perish,
would it matter? —Not at all.

103

El niño negro

Jugaban en la plazoleta

Con una alegría de asueto,

Violetamente menores,

Las turbas solares: chicuelos.

¡Cómo hacia la luz resaltaba,

Condenado de nacimiento

Que aun no ve ni sombras ni muros,

El niño todo error tan negro,

Todavía criatura firme,

No imagen cruel del espejo!

The Negro Child

The street crowd, violently

minor, played in the square,

with the joy of midday

respite. How he stood out

against the light, by birth

condemned, who not yet

sees shadows or walls,

the black child all error,

still a fine firm lad   105

not a mirror's cruel image!

Los atracadores

Boston. Sábado por la mañana. Gran vestíbulo de gran hotel. Hilos de novelas se anudan con tanta corrección que no se advierten.

Entre el despacho de flores y el de cigarillos, entre los que observan poco y los que se van con calma, de repente irrumpe . . .

Ágil, veloz, tajante, una cuadrilla. Se sitúan en sus puntos de eficacia los enmascarados. A la agresión multiplica la estupefacción.

Ya el cajero entrega los miles de dólares de la semana. Nadie chista. Ya los atracadores huyen sobre cálculos de fuga.

Huyen, huyen, huyen con sus Monedas y se precipitan hacia el Óptimo Fin los más desesperadamente burgueses, los tan apresurados.

No se atienen a reglas, las violan. ¡Con tal vigor asumen las ambiciones de todos: Dinero hacia Vida Confortable!

The Holdup Men

Boston. Saturday morning. Lobby of a great
hotel. Threads of novels tied together so
expertly they are hardly apparent.

Between the flower stand and the cigarette counter,
between those who observe little and those who take
their exit calmly, there erupts . . .

Agile, swift, brutal, a gang. The masked men
efficiently take their appointed places. Stupefaction
increases the aggression.

The cashier turns over thousands, the week's
receipts. Not a sound is uttered. The holdup men
escape in their calculated flight.

They flee, they flee, the desperately bourgeois, the
so-hurried gangsters, toward the Optimum Good.

They care not for rules, they violate them. Thus,
so vigorously, the holdup men adopt the
ambitions of us all: Money toward
the Comfortable Life!

El engaño a los ojos

Con qué nobleza se revuelven
Todos juntos esos muchachos
Y claman por una justicia
Perturbando, vociferando,
Tan inocentes los carrillos,
Tan fieros el porte y los pasos,
Con la mirada en dirección
De un porvenir extraordinario,
Pero a la vista ahora, ahora,
Presente ya sobre el asfalto
De las calles estimuladas
Por los rumores calculados
De esa tan filial muchedumbre,
Coro de gargantas y brazos,
Crédulamente fiel y dócil
—Candor por alud—al dictado
De los mayores en edad,
En crueldad y en aparato,
Aun carceleros de una cárcel
Donde todo queda murado,
Sin salida a ningún futuro:
Ni a ese que van anhelando
Los que, por fin, desfilan, jóvenes,
Magníficos, frente al tirano.

The Eyes' Deceit

How nobly they throng together
clamoring for justice, those young men
raising high their voices, inciting and
disturbing, so innocent their faces,
proud their steps and bearing,
their eyes seeking a superb,
a shining future, but right now
within their view, on the asphalt
of streets rocked by the calculated
clamor of the adolescent mob,
chorus of throats and arms,
naïvely faithful and docile
—candorous avalanche—at the bidding of
their elders, superiors in
cruelty and machinations, still
jailers of a prison that encircles
all, without escape to any future:
not even the one they long for,
those who, splendid in their youth,
parade at last before the tyrant.

Aire con época

El aire en la avenida
Se ensancha hacia un espacio
Donde se nos inscriben —fugazmente—
Humos, y serpeando forman letras
Que a todos nos anuncian
Algo con ambición de maravilla.

Comercio, magia, fábula:
En los escaparates nos seducen
Nobles metamorfosis.
La luz es tan veloz
Que un rayo poseído
Nos bastaría para llegar a . . .

Nada persiste lejos.
Un avión arroja a nuestra oreja
Rumores de motores. ¡Rutas nítidas!
Bajo tales poderes
El Globo es una bola bien jugada.
¡Muchos, los juegos! La pasión aprieta
Compacta multitud en ese estadio
Pueril,
Y jugando se asciende hasta las nieves
De blancura feroz
Sobre sus picos vírgenes.

Nada es ajeno al hombre:
Abrazo planetario.
"La luna está muy cerca . . ."

Air of Our Time

The air on the avenue
widens toward a space
where smoke is fleetingly
inscribed and serpentizes letters
that announce to us all
a pretense of marvel.

Commerce, magic, fable:
shop-windows seduce us
by noble metamorphoses.
Light so swift
a desperate ray
would carry us to . . .

III

Nothing lasts long.
A plane flings its roar
at our ears. Lustrous routes!
With such power
the Globe is a well-struck
cue ball.
Many, the games! Passion seizes
a compact mass in the puerile
stadium,
and playing we ascend
to snows of ferocious whiteness
on virgin peaks.

Nothing is foreign to man.
Planetary embrace.
"The moon is near."

¿Algún fin de semana en el satélite?
¿O en Marte?
Junto a las nubes leo: Todo es ya posible.

Por alta mar, redondo el horizonte,
Van volando triunfantes radiogramas
Sin proeza, sin énfasis.
El aire nos trasmite
La historia del minuto.
¡Hoy, hoy!
Un hoy real, muy rico,
Más fuerte que el ayer, de pronto pálido.
La existencia se alarga y te saluda,
Ninfa Penicilina,
A la cabeza de tu coro ilustre,
Coro de salvación.

La edad . . .
              ¡Qué joven: sólo cincuenta años!
Y en un otoño con las hojas secas
Cayeron ilusiones —y sus barbas.
Rasurados semblantes
Mandan, se nos imponen.
La vida se desnuda. Los agostos
Descubren
Playas, pieles gozosamente olímpicas.
Leo sobre las olas:
Aire a tu vivir. Posible, todo.

Weekend on a satellite?
Or perhaps on Mars?
In the clouds I read: all is possible now.

High seas and curved horizons,
triumphant cablegrams fly
gracelessly.
Air transmits to us
the minute's history.
Today! today!
A real today, rich,
mightier than yesterday, suddenly pale.
Existence lengthens and salutes you,
O nymph Penicillin,
chief of your illustrious chorus,
chorus of salvation.

The age . . .
            How young! but fifty years!
And one autumn with dry leaves
hopes fell . . . with their beards.
Shorn features
now command, impose themselves.
Life undresses. Augusts
reveal
beaches, joyfully Olympic skin.
I read on the waves:
air your living. All is possible.

Las olas dicen ... Algo me proponen
Susurrando o gritando alrededor
Infinitos agentes.
Productos y políticas
Me invaden, me obsesionan,
Me aturden
Y se me enredan entre pies y oídos.
¡Socorro!
Van fundiéndose en masa
De alelamiento muchos
Inocentes. Y, dóciles,
Sonríen,
Dispuestos a comprar, a bien morir.
Creer es siempre dulce.

Se elevan edificios
De casi abstractos bloques,
Se vive entre papeles
Con sellos. (Cinco, las fotografías
De cara,
Y cinco de perfil. ¿Soy de los malos?)

Quieren flotar ideas
Entre la luz y el viento. Mala suerte:
Se me desploman sobre mis dos hombros.
Tropiezo con un "...ismo."
Salientes, más allá,
Otros "ismos" atacan
A la vez, importunan,
Estorban. Se me estrechan,

The waves say . . . Something is offered
whispering or shouting about
infinite agents.
Products and politics
invade me, obsess me,
stun me,
and entangle feet and ears.
Help!
Innocents are dissolved
in a stupid mass. And
docile
they smile,
disposed to die, to buy well.
It's sweet to believe.

Buildings arise
in almost abstract block,
we live among stamped
papers. (Five photos
front and as many
profile. Am I of the evil ones?)

Ideas try to waft
between light and wind. Bad luck:
they crumble on my shoulders.
I stumble on an *ism*.
Jutting out beyond
other *isms* attack,
importune,
disturb. Roads, though

Aunque siempre futuros, los caminos.
Leo en el aire: Nada es imposible.

"Libertad" suena a falso
Con retintín ridículo.
Hay dogmas entre bombas. ¡Dogmas, bombas!
Una sola doctrina
Por entre los cadáveres se erige.
Entre las azucenas opiniones
Se mustian, olvidadas.
Hay campos dolorosos
En espirales de concentración.

Entrañas estremece,
Ante los impasibles comadrones,
La gesta maternal.
Yo espero. Toda afirmación me afirma.

Y mientras, esos átomos . . .
Entre los brillos de la calle vaga
Sin figura un tormento.
¿Qué señas nos esbozan esas nubes?
¿Se trata de vivir —o de morir?

always future, become narrow.
I read in the air: Nothing impossible.

"Liberty" sounds false,
a discordant jingle.
Dogmas among bombs. Dogmas,
bombs! A single doctrine
emerges between corpses.
Among the lilies
opinions wither, forgotten.
There are dolorous camps
in concentric spirals.

Entrails tremble
before impassive midwives,
the maternal gesture.
I hope.   Every affirmation affirms me.

And meanwhile, those atoms . . .
Among the street's glitter wanders
a faceless storm.
What signs are read in the clouds?
Is it a question of living . . . or of dying?

Pared

¿Quién ha trazado sobre la pared figuras, palabras
que quieren ser obscenas, y por eso lo son, y
escandalosas, con voluntad provocativa?

¿Qué artista evoca, provoca, convoca desde su
caverna con esos balbuceos rupestres, y a qué
hombre cavernario se dirigen?

¿A qué hora de soledad acaso nocturna, en qué
paréntesis de fugitivo pudo ceder un lápiz a la
obsesión del obseso y solicitar, precisar?

¿Cómo pasa invisible, sin nombre ni semblante,
por qué jamás es sorprendido ese tan solo, tras
la puerta reservada a los "Caballeros?"

¿Llegará a ser cuerdo o lo parecerá en los restantes
días el extraviado confidente? ¿Cuál será su
existencia cotidiana?

¿Qué vida inconfesable, qué dolor y delirio, qué
absurdos, qué esperanzas —las últimas— están
latiendo en esa confidencia de infeliz?

Writing on the Wall

Who could have traced on the wall these figures,
words which want to be obscene (and therefore are)
and scandalous, with provocative desire?

What artist evokes, provokes, convokes from his
cave with these rupestrine stammerings, and to
what primeval man are they addressed?

At what hour of perhaps nocturnal solitude, in what
fugitive parenthesis could a pencil yield to the
obsession of the obsessed, and solicit, define?

How does he pass invisible, nameless and without
countenance, why is his solitude never surprised
across the door reserved for "Gentlemen"?

Will the erring confidant regain his reason, or
seem to, in his remaining days? Of what sort is
his daily existence?

What unutterable secrets, what misery and delirium,
what absurd flights, what hopes—the last—are
beating in this exile's confession?

Hormiga sola

Grande, negra, la hormiga

Se para, bulto inerme

Que de pronto se arroja con sus prisas

A un curso que ya nunca se detiene,

Y como atolondrada zigzaguea,

Corre más regresando y sin oriente,

Por el camino de ninguno busca,

Losas conquista y pierde,

Aumenta su negror con su veloz tamaño,

Veloz, veloz, a solas con su suerte.

Ant Alone

Great and black, the ant
pauses, defenseless bulk
that suddenly resumes in haste
its course that will be endless,
and zigzags scatterbrained,
runs, doubles back, lost and starless,
gains and loses boulders;
whose blackness grows with hurried gait,
swift, eager, alone with its antlike fate.   121

Del trascurso

Miro hacia atrás, hacia los años, lejos,
Y se me ahonda tanta perspectiva
Que del confín apenas sigue viva
La vaga imagen sobre mis espejos.

Aun vuelan, sin embargo, los vencejos
En torno de unas torres, y allá arriba
Persiste mi niñez contemplativa.
Ya son buen vino mis viñedos viejos.

Fortuna adversa o próspera no auguro.
Por ahora me ahinco en mi presente,
Y aunque sé lo que sé, mi afán no taso.

Ante los ojos, mientras, el futuro
Se me adelgaza delicadamente,
Más difícil, más frágil, más escaso.

Of the Passing

I look backward, toward the distant time
and the perspective deepens more and more.
There is scarce a trace of the far confines,
and of their vague image in my mirrors.

The gentle martins, however, still soar
around some towers, and the outline
of my contemplative childhood endures.
Still my old vineyards yield good wine.

I augur future neither dark nor fair.
I cling to my present, and though myself
I know, I do not limit my desire.

Meanwhile, before my eyes, my future wanes,
thins and dwindles delicately,
more difficult, more fragile, more spare.

Ciervos sobre una pared

(Lascaux)

Emergen, se adelantan, vibran
Sobre una pared de la cueva
—A través de siglos y siglos
Profundizados en tiniebla
De inmóvil silencio recóndito
Qui ni la historia misma altera—
Los ciervos, los ciervos en fuga,
En fuga por un friso apenas
Contemplado y ya resurrecto
Sobre millones de horas muertas,
Fuga y su desfile de friso
Vivaz hacia más primavera.
Uno tras otro siguen juntos
Alzando siempre las cabezas
Adorablemente alargadas
Tras una vaguedad de meta.
Refrenado palpita el ímpetu
Que bosques y bosques desea.
Al perfil otorgan, nervioso,
Aireación las cornamentas,
Y hasta se percibe el susurro
De las soledades inciertas.
Vibrando resaltan los ciervos.
En su vida sin muerte quedan.

Deer on a Wall

(LASCAUX)

They emerge, go forward,
vibrate on the cave's wall
—across centuries and
centuries, sunken in a
fog of still recondite
silence that not even
History alters—the stags,
stags in flight, in flight on
a frieze hardly discerned,
resurrected now on
millions of dormant hours,
the flight and their painted
procession vigorously
toward a new springtime.
They follow one after
another, raising high
their gently lengthened heads
toward a goal's vagueness.
The checked force beats, impetus
that thirsts for more and more
forest. The horns grant the
wind's movement to the nervous
profiles, and there is heard
a murmur of uncertain
solitudes. The deer loom
vibrantly. In their
deathless life they remain.

Tréboles

(1)

Erudito: ¿por qué me explotas?
¿Mis cielos se encuentran abajo,
Por entre esas nubes de notas?

(2)

Tengo un capricho de Goya:
"El dictador cree en Dios."
Como de su Dios va en pos,
En muchos muertos se apoya.

(3)

¿No es muy humano que rimen,
A fuerza de tanta fuerza,
Bomba y paz, justicia y crimen?

(4)

¡Si yo no soy puro en nada,
Y menos en poesía!
Si ser hombre es todavía
La flor de nuestra jornada!

Clover Leaves

(1)

Why do you exploit me, learned dolt?
Is my heaven found down there,
among those fuzzy clouds of notes?

(2)

Here's Goya's *Capricho* with the line:
"The Dictator believes in God."
On the piled bodies of the dead
he climbs in search of the divine.

(3)

How human that they should rhyme:
(by dint of so much force)
bomb and peace, justice and crime.

(4)

I am not pure in anything
and least of all in poetry.
To learn to be a man is still
the terminus of our journey.

(5)

Un caballo junto al mar.

Crines, oleaje, viento.

¿Qué fábula va a estallar?

(6)

Se ha convertido. Con furia

Reniega de su pasado,

Y con furia nos injuria:

Somos aún su pecado.

(5)

A horse beside the sea.
Mane, waves and wind.
What fable will burst free?

(6)

He has converted. With din
he rages against his past,
us he assaults with bombast:
we who are still his sin.

Despertar español

¡Oh blanco muro de España!

—Federico García Lorca

I

¿Dónde estoy?
　　　　Me despierto en mis palabras,
Por entre las palabras que ahora digo,
A gusto respirando
Mientras con ellas soy, del todo soy
Mi nombre,
Y por ellas estoy con mi paisaje:
Aquellos cerros grises de la infancia,
O ese incógnito mar, ya compañero
Si mi lengua le nombra, le somete.

No estoy solo. ¡Palabras!

Y merced a sus signos
Puedo acotar un trozo de planeta
Donde vivir tratando de entenderme
Con prójimos más próximos
En la siempre difícil tentativa
De gran comunidad.

A través de un idioma
¿Yo podría llegar a ser el hombre
Por fin humano a que mi esfuerzo tiende
Bajo este sol de todos?

Spanish Awakening

O white wall of Spain!

—Federico García Lorca

I

Where am I?
        I wake in my words,
among the words I speak now,
breathing gladly while they are by me, I am
my name utterly,
and through them to my landscape:
those grey hills of my childhood
or that unknown sea, companion
if my tongue names and masters it.

I am not alone. Words!

And thanks to their signs
I can mark off a piece of the planet
where I may live attempting to speak
with my near, my fellow men
in the always difficult endeavor
of community.

With the aid of my language
could I aspire to be that man
at last human toward whom my hand reaches
beneath this common sun?

Ay patria,
Con malos padres y con malos hijos,
O tal vez nada más desventurados
En el gran desconcierto de una crisis
Que no se acaba nunca,
Esa contradicción que no nos deja
Vivir nuestro destino,
A cuestas cada cual
Con el suyo en un ámbito despótico . . .
Ay, patria,
Tan anterior a mí,
Y que yo quiero, quiero
Viva después de mí —donde yo quede
Sin fallecer en frescas voces nuevas
Que habrán de resonar hacia otros aires,
Aires con una luz
Jamás, jamás anciana.
Luz antigua tal vez sobre los muros
Dorados
Por el sol de un octubre y de su tarde:
Reflejos
De muchas tardes que no se han perdido,
Y alumbrarán los ojos de otros hombres
—Quién sabe— y sus hallazgos.

III

¡Fluencia!
Y nunca se interrumpe,
Y nunca llega al mar

Ah, fatherland,
bad fathers and worse sons,
or perhaps merely unfortunates
in the vast disorder of a crisis
never ending,
that contradiction which prevents us
from living out our destiny,
each man bearing his fate on his back
in a despotic zone . . .
Ah fatherland,
so prior to my being,
that I love and want
to live after me—where I may remain
deathless in fresh new voices
that will resound toward other airs
airs with a never
ancient light.
An antique light perhaps on walls
gilded
by an October sun and its decline:
reflections
of many afternoons unlost
that will kindle the eyes of other men
perhaps, and their discoveries.

III

A flowing!
And it never ceases
never runs down to the sea

Ni sabe de traiciones.
Río de veras fiel a su mandato,
A su fatal avance sesgo a sesgo,
Rumbo a la primavera con su estío,
Y en las agudas barcas
Las eternas parejas
De nuevo amor.
   Y no hay más mundo que ése.

Un mundo bajo soles
Y nuestra voluntad.

Paso ha de abrirse por las nuevas sangres
Incógnito futuro
Libérrimo.
¿Vamos a él? Él es quien nos arrastra
Rehaciendo el presente
Fugaz
Mientras confluye todo por su curso
De cambio y permanencia,
España, España, España.

IV

Nuestra invención y nuestro amor, España,
Pese a los pusilánimes,
Pese a las hecatombes—bueyes muertos—
Sobre las tierras yermas,
Entre ruinas y fábulas
Con luces de ponientes
Hacia noches y auroras.

knows nothing of treasons.
River true to its mandate,
to its fatal thrusting advance
toward Spring with its Summer
and in the narrow boats
the eternal couples
of a new love.
                    And there is no other world.

A world beneath suns
and our will.

It must make its way through new blood
toward an unknown future
utterly free.
Shall we set out? It carries us along
remaking the present
fugitive
while all converges in its course
of permanence and change,
Spain, Spain, Spain.

IV

Our invention, our love, Spain,
in spite of the pusillanimous
in spite of the hecatombs—the slaughtered cattle—
on the barren earth,
among ruins and fables
with sunset's light
toward nights and dawns.

Y todo, todo en vilo,
En aire
De nuestra voluntad.

Queremos más España.
Esa incógnita España no más fácil
De mantener en pie
Que el resto del planeta,
Atractiva entre manos escultoras
Como nunca lo es bajo los odios,
Creación sobre un trozo de universo
Que vale más ahondado que dejado.

136

¿Península? No basta geografía.
Queremos un paisaje con historia.

v

Errores y aflicciones.
            ¡Cuántas culpas!
Gran historia es así:
Realidad hay, compacta.

En el recuerdo veo un muro blanco,
Un sol que se recrea
Difundiéndose en ocio
Para el contemplativo siempre en obra.

¡Blanco muro de España!
No quiero saber más.

And all ascending
in the air
of our will.

We will, we want more Spain.

That unknown Spain no easier
to keep afloat
than the rest of the planet
captivating amid sculpting hands
as never beneath hatreds,
creation upon a piece of universe
better sunken than abandoned.

Peninsula? Geography is not enough.
Let history join our landscape.

v

Errors and afflictions.
                    Unending guilt.
Great history: compact reality.

In memory I see a white wall
a sun that takes its ease
leisurely spreading itself
for the pensive at labor.

White wall of Spain!
I would know no more.

Se me agolpa la vida hacia un destino,
Ahí,
Que el corazón convierte en voluntario.

¡Durase junto al muro!

Y no me apartarán vicisitudes
De la fortuna varia.
¡Tierno apego sin término!
Blanco muro de España, verdadera:
Nuestro pacto es enlace en la verdad.

138

Life thrusts me toward a destiny,
there,
which the heart transmutes into choice.

May I remain beside that wall!

And vicissitudes of fortune
will not separate me.
Tender, endless passion!
White wall of Spain, exact Spain:
our pact the truest union.

La afirmación humana

(ANNA FRANK)

En torno el crimen absoluto. Vulgo,
El vulgo más feroz,
En un delirio de vulgaridad
Que llega a ser demente,
Se embriaga con sangre,
La sangre de Jesús.
Y cubre a los osarios
Una vergüenza universal: a todos,
A todos nos sonroja.
¿Quién, tan extenso el crimen,
No sería culpable?

La noche sufre de inocencia oculta.

Y en esa noche tú, por ti alborada,
A un cielo con sus pájaros tan próxima,
A pesar del terror y del ahogo,
Sin libertad ni anchura,
Amas, inventas, creces
En ámbito de pánico,
Que detener no logra tus esfuerzos
Tan enérgicamente diminutos
De afirmación humana:
Con tu pueblo tu espíritu
—Y el porvenir de todos.

Human Affirmation

(ANNE FRANK)

Around her absolute crime. The mob,
that bestial mob,
in a delirium of vulgarity
that ascends to madness,
gets drunk with blood,
the blood of Jesus.
And a universal shame
blankets the charnel house:
the shame is ours, yours and mine.
When the crime is so far-ranging
who can be free of guilt?

Night suffers from hidden innocence.

And in that night (for your sake made dawn,
so near the singing of birds),
in spite of the terror and affliction,
your every movement constrained,
you love, you invent, you grow
in a terrain of panic
which your vibrant diminutive strength
of human affirmation
cannot hold back:
your spirit rests with your people
—and the future of us all.

Trágico, no absurdo

(ALBERT CAMUS)

I

El coche va corriendo, sutilmente veloz,
Hacia una meta
   —¿meta?—
      que lo aspira y fascina
—Cuidado—
   sin cesar.
      La ruta es una hoz
—Cuidado con el filo—de amenaza muy fina.

II

¡Cuerpo veloz!
   De pronto
      —¿suerte ciega?—
        lo absorbe
Todo un soplo mortal. ¿Absurdo, falso el orbe?

III

La física ajustaba las ruedas al camino.
Guiaba el conductor según su pensamiento.
Se sumían las cosas en afán violento.
Un error. Ay, la ley. Ni milagro ni sino.

Tragic, not Absurd

(ALBERT CAMUS)

The car, subtly swift, hurries toward a goal
—goal or magnet—
         that draws and entrances
—take care!—
       endlessly.
              The road is a scythe
—beware of its edge—finely threatening.

II   143

Rapid forms!
      Suddenly
           —blind fate?—
                    he is hurled
by a mortal breath. Absurd, false the world?

III

Physical laws ordered the wheels to the road.
The driver followed the drift of his thoughts. Straight-
way all was consumed by a violent thrust. An
error. The world's law. Neither portent, nor fate.

Vida concreta

La oscuridad y el silencio son una masa negativa
que, sin embargo, cubre, pesa y me protege a mí,
casi indistinto de la noche en un mundo que casi
ignoro, apenas recordándome.

El silencio va convirtiéndose en zumbido difuso
como energía del negror donde sigo, entre hilachas
de imágenes que tal vez esté soñando: blanda
conciencia de aún molusco y ya persona.

Está resquebrajándose por crecientes rendijas
la mole nocturna, y el zumbido general es a veces
rumor de rumores que se arrastran, que ya ruedan.
Una ciudad. Vehículos.

El tiempo vaga sin precisión de horario. Apunta
en la memoria una desnudez, la carne de un alba
que se colorea. La esbozo yo, también esbozado
por la conciencia y el mundo.

Acaba por disiparse la compartida inmensidad.
Un pregón de trapero me hinca en historia. Suma
plenitud: la más concreta. "Cenciaioo!" Las
siete. Calle florentina . . . Y yo, por fin.

Concrete Life

The darkness and silence are a negative mass which, nevertheless, covers and protects me, I who am indistinct from the night, in a world I hardly know, in which I can hardly recognize myself.

The silence gradually becomes a diffuse hum, like the energy of a blackness in which I am, among fragments of images that perhaps I dream: the bland consciousness, still mollusk, yet already person.

The nocturnal mass is slowly breaking up, its surface cleaving and splitting, and the general hum is at times the noise of noises that drag, that roll. A city. Vehicles.

Time wanders without help of clocks, of schedules. Memory contains a hint of nakedness, the flesh of dawn that takes shape. I sketch it, I who am in turn outlined by consciousness and world.

The shared immensity finally dissipates. A rag buyer returns me to history. The highest plenitude: the most concrete. *Cenciaioo!* Seven o'clock. A Florentine street . . . And I, at last.

Gatos de Roma

Los gatos,
No vagabundos pero sin dueño,
Al sol adormecidos
En calles sin aceras,
O esperando una mano dadivosa
Tal vez por entre ruinas,
Los gatos,
Inmortales de modo tan humilde,
Retan al tiempo, duran
Atravesando las vicisitudes,
Sin saber de la Historia
Que levanta edificios
O los deja abismarse entre pedazos
Bellos aún, ahora apoyos nobles
De esas figuras: libres.
Mirada fija de unos ojos verdes
En soledad, en ocio y luz remota.
Entrecerrados ojos,
Rubia la piel y calma iluminada.
Erguido junto a un mármol,
Superviviente resto de columna,
Alguien feliz y pulcro
Se atusa con la pata relamida.
Gatos. Frente a la Historia,
Sensibles, serios, solos, inocentes.

The Cats of Rome

The cats,
not vagabonds but ownerless,
sleeping in the sun
in streets without sidewalks,
or waiting for a generous hand,
perhaps, among the ruins,
the cats,
so humbly immortal,
challenge time, persist
through vicissitudes,
know nothing of history
which raises edifices
or lets them crumble to pieces
that are still beautiful, now the noble supports
of these figures: free.
The fixed stare of green eyes
in solitude, in leisure and distant light.
Half-open eyelids,
blond fur and illumined calm.
Erect beside marble,
surviving remains of a column,
a comely and happy someone
spruces himself with wet paw.
Cats. Before History,
sensitive, serious, alone, innocent.

El asesino del planeta

Alguien podría ser este asesino. Tal vez se halla
ahora soñando con el desenlace grandioso que
satisfaría un instinto muy radical desde la entraña
de la más ilustre de las bestias,

Esa bestia que algunas veces consigue trepar hasta
un nivel humano. El Sumo Desposorio podría
consumarse: instinto de muerte con apocalipsis.
—¡Te quiero, te destruyo, mi planeta!

Nuestro asesino no es, por supuesto, el Demonio
encarnado ni el Mal en persona. Mediocre, eso sí.
Y vulgar como todo el mundo a sus horas de televisión,
de pornografía. ¿Cruel?

Cruel en potencia acaso. Bien vestido. Un señor.
Y técnico. ¿De burocracia, de política, de guerra?
Un técnico subalterno con deberes en despachos, en
edificios oficiales.

Así, amasado con abstracciones, nutrido de papel
y de número, sujeto dócilmente a la ficción sin
imaginación, sordo a la ironía, el hombre se hunde
en irrealidad, en su irrealidad.

The Planet's Assassin

Someone could be that assassin. Perhaps even now he is
dreaming of the grandiose dénouement that would
satisfy a radical instinct in the depths of that
most illustrious of beasts,

that beast which at times manages to ascend to a human
level. The Highest Marriage would be consummated:
death instinct with apocalypse.
"I love you, I destroy you, my Planet!"

Our assassin is not, of course, the Devil incarnate
or Evil in person. Mediocre, rather. And common as
anyone in his hours of television, of pornography. Is
he cruel?

Latently, perhaps. Well-dressed. A gentleman. And
technician. Of bureaucracy, politics, war? A
subordinate technician, invested with duties in offices,
government edifices.

Thus, kneaded with abstractions, nourished by papers
and numbers, docilely subject to fiction without
imagination, deaf to irony, the man plunges into
unreality, his unreality.

Un vacío. Y de pronto, al borde de ese vacío
el poder. Conclusión: ¡si el poder invadiera ese
vacío, si el vacío se fundiese con el poder! La
mano del mediocre sobre la Manivela.

El poder, mucho más fuerte que los más potentes,
juega a la utopía, a la cruzada, alumbra antorchas
entre pirámides de negocios. ¿Y si los átomos
desencadenaran su científico furor?

Nunca faltan pretextos. Un avión derribado,
una frontera violada, el honor de ... ¿El honor?
El honor del país. ¡Oh libertad, oh comunidad!
Todos cierran los ojos. Y la catástrofe.

Suicidio planetario, pureza del no ser. O por
odio. Y como experimento. Los hombres han
convertido en acto siempre toda sobrehumana
o inhumana posibilidad: una especie de destino.

Las bombas están ahí y aguardan su plenitud.
Los medios pesan más que los fines. Y tú, mediocre
asesino en potencia máxima, ¿vencerás a todos
nuestros dioses juntos?

An emptiness. And suddenly, at the edge of emptiness, power. Conclusion: if power were to invade that emptiness, if nothingness became fused with power! The hand of mediocre man on the Lever.

Power far stronger than potentates plays with utopias and crusades, kindles torches amidst industrial pyramids. And if the Atoms were to let loose their scientific furor?

Never a lack of pretexts. A fallen plane, a border violated, the honor of ... Honor? Of the country. Oh freedom, oh community! Everyone closes their eyes. And the catastrophe.

Planetary suicide, purity of non-being. Or for hatred. And as an experiment. Man has converted every superhuman and subhuman possibility into an act: a kind of destiny.

The bombs are there and await their plenitude. The means weigh more heavily than the end. And you, mediocre assassin to the Nth degree, will you overcome all of our gods together?

Clamor estrellado

Ruido, una red de ruido, va envolviendo el planeta
en que las explosiones y los disparos y los murmullos
se funden a quejidos, gritos, alaridos bajo una
luz que calla.

La luz se retrae y la batahola se refugia
atenuándose en la menor realidad de lo oscuro,
que ampara a todos, amantes, dolientes, esforzados
en plenitud, en crisis, en espera.

Continúa siempre el esfuerzo, sin interrumpirse
dolor ni amor, durante la tregua cotidiana
entre el sueño y la sombra, cuando casi no
existe para el insomne el signo sonoro.

Arriba, las luces tan remotas no saben del hombre
que las contempla, confortado por la paz en que
se resuelven esos procesos violentísimos, esas
llamas de creación.

Creación que mal afronta la mente, inmensidad
de astros y siglos nada vertiginosos para ese
mar nocturno que surcan—como este planeta,
entre constelaciones sumido en el silencio.

Shattered Clamor

Noise, a net of noise envelops the planet, in which
explosions, shots and murmurs fuse into laments, cries
and howls beneath a silent light.

The light withdraws and the hubbub takes refuge,
narrowing into the least reality of the dark, that shelters
all, lovers, the sick, the vigorous, in crisis, expectant.

The effort goes on, pain and love without interruption,
during that daily truce between dreams and darkness,
when the sonorous sign hardly exists for the insomniac.

Above, the so-remote lights know nothing of man that
contemplates them, man who is comforted by the
peace in which those violent processes,
the flames of creation, are resolved.

Creation which the mind conceives with difficulty,
immensity of stars and centuries not dizzying to that
nocturnal sea which they furrow—like this planet,
swallowed by silence amid constellations.

Part III: from *Homenaje*

Al margen de los Browning

> *From Casa Guidi windows*
> *I looked forth ...*
>
> —E. B. B.

Florencia, Via Maggio tras un puente,
Puente de Santa Trinità,
Y al final de la calle Casa Guidi.
Y allí los dos poetas
Valientemente, peligrosamente
Viven y se desviven
Por convertir sus sueños en su vida
Real, la cotidiana:
Elizabeth y Robert,
El gran amor, silencio, verso, prosa,
La prosa tan difícil de los diálogos
A viva voz sin arte,
Y en la ciudad que es la ciudad soñada,
Realísima y bellísima
Con hermosura siempre verdadera.
Los años amontonan
Sus materiales brutos,
Que habrá de atravesar, y sin embustes,
La luz del corazón y de la mente.
Fugas no habrá ni vanas ilusiones.
Los amantes se afrontan día a día.
O freedom! O my Florence!

156

On the Margin of the Brownings

Love and Valor

*From Casa Guidi windows
I looked forth . . .*

—E. B. B.

Florence, Via Maggio across a bridge,
the bridge of Santa Trinità,
and at the end of the street Casa Guidi.
There the two poets
valiantly, dangerously,
live and strive
to make everyday life
of the stuff of their dreams.
Elisabeth and Robert,
their love, silence, verse, prose,
difficult prose of the dialogues
viva voce, artlessly,
and the city, the dreamt-of city,
real and most beautiful
without end.
The years heap up
their crude matter
that the mind's, the heart's light
will cross unflinchingly.
No flights, no vain illusions.
The lovers confront each other
day by day.
O freedom! O my Florence!

Al margen de Henry James

La musa retirada

"The Aspern Papers"

La musa retirada,
Retirada en retiro de recuerdos,
Vive reinando sola en su pasado,
Insigne entre el amor
—Tan suyo, tan secreto noche a noche—
Y las palabras de la poesía,
Pública al fin, ya célebre.

¿Fue quizás el fantasma
De un hombre que soñase
Con la belleza purificadora?
Allí está. No es ficción. No es un concepto.
En su palacio, junto al agua viva,
Es ella siempre: musa
—Con un alma en su carne—
Del verso que volando desde un nido
Asciende hasta su cúspide,
Más allá de los bosques olvidados.

Los poemas, las cartas y en su reino
La mujer para siempre ya reinante.

On the Margin of Henry James

THE RETIRED MUSE

"The Aspern Papers"

The retired muse
in withdrawal full of memories
lives reigning alone in her past
splendent amid her love
(hers, in nightly secret)
and the words, those poetic words,
made public, at last renowned.

Was it perhaps the ghost
of a man who dreamed
a purifying beauty?
There it is. Not fiction. Nor abstraction.
In her palace, beside the live water,
is she forever: muse
—soul in her flesh—
of the verse which flying from its nest
ascends to mountain peak,
beyond the forgotten forests.

The poems, letters, and in her kingdom
a woman always queen of her domain.

159

Al margen de Santayana

Huesped de hotel

> *preserving my essential character of*
> *stranger and traveller, with the*
> *philosophic freedom ...*

I

Entre desconocidos que le ignoran,
Solterón casi siempre solitario,
Vive—sin convivir—con extranjeros,
Mínimo alrededor acompañante.
Si rentista feliz, perfecto artista.

II

De incógnito caudillo de monólogo,
Pensamiento cabal, amor frustrado,
Independiente en orden, serio ambiguo,
Huésped de un astro, rumbo hacia la nada.

III

A la materia con su fe se asoma,
Y español de raíz, inglés de idioma,
Entre las soledades de su cima,
Libre de lazos, palpa el mundo lego,
Sin dioses. La verdad le da sosiego.

On the Margin of Santayana

Hotel Guest

> *preserving my essential character of*
> *stranger and traveller, with the*
> *philosophic freedom . . .*

I

Among unfamiliar faces who ignore him,
the always solitary bachelor,
he lives—not with, among—strangers,
the least companionship he requires.
Of independent means; perfect artist.

II

Incognito, proud prince of monologue,
flawless in thought, in love frustrated.
Orderly, detached, ambiguously grave,
guest on a star drifting toward Nothing.

III

With his faith he peers out at Matter
and, deep-rooted Spaniard, English-tongued,
among the solitudes of his lofty peaks,
unfettered, he explores the secular cosmos,
the godless. Truth gives him repose.

Federico García Lorca

También recordando a Miguel Hernández

I

Un murmullo cruzando va el silencio
Con fluencia continua,
Manantial que es un alba sobre rocas,
Vislumbres sobre espumas.
¿En el agua vacila una mirada?
Un esclarecimiento va aguzándose
Como si fuera ya radioso espíritu,
Y ya tiende hacia un canto,
Que dice . . .
                    Dice: vida.
Nada más.
              Invasión
De evidencias nos sume, nos asume
Y sin embriagarnos, convincente,
Nos arrebata a un aire—luz. Se impone
La suma desnudez irrebatible.
Estalla claridad,
Claridad que es humana
Con su luz de conquista,
Avance de una forma,
De un gesto que es lenguaje,
Triunfo de creador,
Y con duende, con ángel y con musa,
Luminosos espectros,

Federico García Lorca

Dedicated also to the memory of
Miguel Hernández

I

A murmur crosses the silence
with a continual flowing,
a source like dawn among rocks
glimmers above seafoam.
Does a human gaze hesitate on water?
An illumination becomes sharper
as if it were radiant spirit
and moves now toward song
which says . . .

163

It says: life.
Nothing more.

An invasion
of evidences presses upon us, uplifts
us, convincing without intoxicating,
carries us to light—air. The clearest,
irrefutable nakedness imposes.
Clarity breaks forth,
clarity that is yet human
with its conquering light
approach of a form,
of a gesture that is language,
a creator's triumph,
and with his angel, his *duende*,* his muse,
luminous specters,

---

* *duende*: a kind of elf or goblin or good attending spirit.

En plenitud coloca
La humanidad del hombre.

II

El hombre sabe lo que ignora el árbol,
Lo que contempla el mar indiferente.
A través de un casual deslumbramiento,
De pronto se descubre . . .
¿Qué se descubre ya?
A zaga de la vida va la muerte:
Sucesión—no hay remedio—rigurosa.

Ved al privilegiado.
¿Libre y gozoso infunde
La dicha de la luz?
Ahora es quien padece
Bajo el rayo sombrío.
Dolor, terror, alarma siempre en guardia.

En las umbrías de este sol cruel,
A pesar de la paz
A plomo de las siestas,
Paredes encaladas son anuncio,
Entre cactos y olivos,
De atropello, de crimen.
Inminencias dañinas,
Ay, precipitarán,
Y violentamente,
La fluencia de sangre hacia un cuchillo
De venganza, de rabia.

he leads into plenitude
the humanness of man.

II

A man knows what the tree does not,
what the sea contemplates indifferently.
Through a casual dazzling light
is suddenly discovered . . .
What?
Behind life comes death along—
there's no cure—a rigorous succession.

Behold the chosen one.
Does he freely, gladly instill
the joy of his light?
Now it is he who suffers
beneath the somber ray.
Pain, terror, alarm always on guard.

165

In the shade of this cruel sun,
in spite of the leaden
peace of siestas,
whitewashed walls are a sign,
among cactus and olives,
of an outrage, a crime.
Baleful imminences
will violently
precipitate
the flowing of blood toward a knife
of vengeance, of rage.

Miradle bien. El es quien mejor sabe
De un derramado carmesí postrero.

III

El campo sometido a su negrura,
Los desiertos del cielo sin sus lumbres,
Ya las ínfimas fuerzas prevalecen,
Dilatan ese caos
Que no prepara a ser.
Caos: un solo mar
De vómitos. Los odios
Buscan razones, hallan más delirios.
Los muertos se extravían en silencio,
Silencio entre descargas.
Sepulturas sin losas.

¿Va a caer el mejor?

Algo brilla un instante,
Y la adivinación no se equivoca:
Excelso. Caerá.

No caerá.
　　　　　¡No!
　　　　　　　¡No!
Ojos había para ver. Caído.

Del estupor, muy largo,
Queda suspenso el orbe.
La desesperación

Observe him well. He knows best
that final crimson outpour.

III

The countryside surrendered to its blackness,
the sky's deserts without their lights,
the vilest forces prevail
and extend that chaos
not ready for being.
Chaos: a single ocean
of vomit. Hatreds
seek reasons, find madness.
The dead wander lost in silence,
silence among shots.
Sepulchers without headstones.

Will the finest fall?

Something glistens momentarily
and the divination does not err:
The best. Shall fall.

He will not.
        No!
          No!
Eyes are there to see. Has fallen.

The world does not recover soon
from its long stupor.
Despair, tearless,

No llora aún, muy seca.
Acompaña, latente,
El invisible cúmulo estrellado.

A corazones entre sí remotos
Se les juntan sus cóleras.
¿A quién no abarca pena universal?
No habrá llanto bastante
Por todos los caídos
Sepultos, insepultos.

La Creación es una destrucción.

168

Hasta el sumo dicente se ha callado.
Inmortal en nosotros, pero muerto.
No hay brisa melancólica entre olivos.
Desesperado viento sobre el muerto.
Desesperado el hombre junto al muerto.

does not weep.
But the invisible starry cumulus
latently accompanies.

Scattered, distant hearts
join their rage.
Who escapes that universal sorrow?
There are not enough tears
for all the fallen,
for the buried, the unburied.

Creation is destruction.

Even the most eloquent is silenced.

Immortal in us, but dead.
There is no melancholy wind among the olive trees.
Only a despairing wind above the dead man.
Despairing man beside the dead.

La gran aventura

Es Dios quien al hombre crea,
O el hombre quien crea a Dios.
Alguien desde una platea
Pregunta: ¿Cuál de estas dos

Creaciones ideales
Más sería maravilla?
—Mucho en ambos casos vales,
Hombre, centella de arcilla.

O tu origen es divino,
Y hay barca, remero y remos,
O Dios en tu mente advino.
Siempre hay creación. La vemos.

¿Que nuestra inquietud perdura?
La Tierra es gran aventura.

The Great Adventure

Was it God Who created man,
or man who created God?
From behind the proscenium
a voice asks: which of these

ideal creations is the more
to be marveled at?
In either case you are
worthy, clay-borne spark, Man.

Either your origin is divine,
and there is boat, oarsman and oar,
or God arose in your mind.
Behold: there is always creation.

Does our disquiet endure?
The Earth is a great adventure.

Cuerpo a solas

Junto a la tumba de M.M.

> Caminantes: callad.
> La hermosa actriz ha muerto,
> Ay, de publicidad.

> Entre fulgor y ruido,
> Aquella desnudez
> Extravió su sentido.

> Era tan observada
> Por los ojos de todos
> Que se escondió en la nada.

> Allí no habrá ya escena
> Donde suene un fatal
> Arrastre de cadena.

> El bello cuerpo yace
> Libre, por fin, a solas.
> ¡Uf!

> Requiescat in pace.

Body Alone

Beside the tomb of M.M.

Travelers: be silent.
The lovely ingénue has died,
alas, of publicity.

Amid the noise and lenses,
that nakedness
took leave of its senses.

She was so much observed
by all of our eyes,
she hid herself in nothingness.

There will be no scene,
over there, with a baleful
dragging of chain.

That beautiful form released,
lies, at last, alone.
Uf!

      Rest in peace.

El cuento de nunca acabar

A mi hijo

El mar, el cielo, fuerzas sin fatiga,
Concurren bajo luz serenadora.
Sólo soy yo en la tarde el fatigado.

Se impone a todos este azul intenso,
Azul tendido hacia su propia calma,
Apenas iniciándose
Variaciones de espuma.
Vagos cuerpos de nubes
Aguardan el crepúsculo y su fiesta.
Mis ojos ven lo que han amado siempre,
Y la visión seduce más ahora,
Frágil bajo penumbras
Que a través, ay, de esta mirada mía
Tienden hacia lo umbrío.
Los años, si me dieron sus riquezas,
Amontonan sus números,
Y siento más veloz
La corriente que fluye arrebatándome
De prisa hacia un final.

No importa. La luz cuenta,
Nos cuenta sin cesar una aventura,
Y no acaba, no acaba:
Desenlace no hay.
Aventura de un sol y de unos hombres.
Todos, al fin extintos,

Story Without End

To my son

The sea, the sky, tireless forces,
concur beneath a serene light.
This afternoon I alone am weary.

This intense blue imposes itself,
a blue inclined toward its own calm,
variations of foam
hardly commencing.
Vague forms of clouds
await the sunset and its frolic.
My eyes see that which they have always loved
and now the familiar vision seduces more,
fragile beneath penumbras
that across this my sight
tends toward the shadowy.
The years, though they gave me their wealth,
pile up their numbers
and I feel more swift
the flowing current carrying me
faster toward my end.

It doesn't matter. The light matters,
it relates ceaselessly an adventure
and it never concludes:
there is no denouement.
Story of the sun and some men.
All, finally extinct,

Se pierden bajo un cielo que los cubre.
El cielo es inmortal.
Feliz quien pasa aquí,
Si este planeta le ha caído en suerte,
Sus efímeros días
Como los del follaje
Que será amarillento.
¿Soy yo más que una hoja
De un árbol rumoroso?
Un destino común
—¿El único?—nos junta en la corteza
De un astro siempre activo,
Todos así partícipes
De un movimiento que conduce a todos
Hacia . . . ¿Tal vez no hay meta?

Ese mundo, que en mí se va perdiendo,
Frente a mí sigue intacto
Con su frescor de fábula.

Un abierto balcón,
Una sombra latente junto al muro
De una calle en la siesta del estío
Calles, ciudades, campos, cielos, luces
Infinitas . . . Y el hombre
Con su poder terrible,
Y en medio de los ruidos,
Por entre los desórdenes innúmeros,
La habitual maravilla de una orquesta.

Una vida no cabe en la memoria.

and lost beneath the sky that covers them.
The sky is immortal.
Happy is he that passes here,
if he has chanced upon this planet,
his ephemeral days
like those of leaves
that will turn yellow.
Am I more than a leaf
of a rustling tree?
A common destiny
(the only one?) unites us on the bark
of an incessantly moving star,
all thus participants
in a thrust that carries us
toward . . . There is perhaps no goal?

That world, slowly waning in me,
still stands intact before me
with all its fabled freshness.

An open balcony,
a latent shadow beside a wall
of a street in summer's siesta,
streets, cities, country, skies, infinite
lights . . . And man
with his terrible power,
in the midst of noises,
among innumerable disorders,
an orchestra's customary marvel.

Memory cannot contain a lifetime.

Ambitos de amistades,
Espíritus sin roce
Con Historia, con público,
La mujer, el amor, las criaturas,
Nuestra existencia en pleno consumada
Entre bienes y males.

Surge una gratitud
¿En cuántas direcciones?
Se despliega la rosa de los vientos.

¡Amigos! Este Globo
Florece bajo diálogos:
Extraordinaria flora
—Mezclándose a la selva
Que nunca se destruye—
Por entre las historias diminutas
Que recatan sin fechas los instantes
Supremos, tan humildes.
La raíz de mi ser los ha guardado
Para abocar al que yo soy. Más rico,
Respirando agradezco.
El hombre entre los hombres,
El sol entre los astros,
¿En torno a una Conciencia?
(Más que una hoja yo no soy, no sé.)

Miro atrás. ¡El olvido me ha borrado
Tanto de lo que fui!
La memoria me oculta sus tesoros.
¿Cómo decir adiós,

Circles of friendship,
spirits who do not brush against
History or public,
a woman, love, children,
our existence fully consummated
among good and evil circumstances.

A gratitude surges
—in how many directions?
The rose of winds unfurls.

Friends! This Globe
flourishes beneath dialogues:
extraordinary flora
(mixed with the never-
    blighted forest)
among the diminutive histories
that hold back, dateless, the supreme,
the humble instants.
My living roots have retained them
to flow into my being. Richer for them,
I breathe in gratitude.
A man among men,
the sun among stars—
that move about a Conscience?
(I do not know whether I am more than a leaf.)

I look backwards. Forgetfulness has erased
so much of what I was!
My memory conceals its treasures.
How to say goodbye,

Final adiós al mundo?
Y nadie se despide de sí mismo,
A no ser en teatro de suicida.
Estar muerto no es nada.
Morir es sólo triste.
Me dolerá dejaros a vosotros,
Los que aquí seguiréis,
Y no participar de vuestra vida.
El cuento no se acaba.
Sólo se acaba quien os cuenta el cuento.

¿Habrá un debe y haber
Que resuma el valor de la existencia,
Es posible un numérico balance?
Ser, vivir, absolutos,
Sacros entre dos nadas, dos vacíos.
El ser es el valor. Yo soy valiendo,
Yo vivo. ¡Todavía!
Tierra bajo mis plantas,
El mar y el cielo con nosotros, juntos.

a final goodbye to the world?
No one takes leave of himself,
save, perhaps, a theatrical suicide.
To be dead is nothing.
To die, that alone is sad.
I will regret to leave you,
you that continue here,
and not participate in your living.
The story is without end.
Only the teller reaches his conclusion.

Is there a plus and a minus
that may resume the value of existence,
is a numerical solution possible?
Being, living are absolute
and sacred between two Nothings, two vacancies.
It is worthy to be. I thus am worthy,
I live. I still live!
Earth beneath my feet,
sea and sky with us, together.

Notes on the Poems

*In these notes the editor occasionally quotes from let-
ters to him from Jorge Guillén; such passages are in
quotation marks and are followed by the initials "J.G."*—
TRANSLATOR'S NOTE.

PART I

Más allá (Beyond):

Más allá (only the first of six parts is here translated) is the key work of *Cántico,* the cornerstone which contains Guillén's major themes. It is a poem of awakening; of emerging from the chaos, the half-death of sleep, to morning, light, and life. It is about the rebirth we experience with each morning. Air, light, being, joy, the moment—the major themes of *Cántico*—are all present in this first part. The light invades his being; the *consistencies* become things, take shape and limit, center him. In the last stanza he says: "Reality invents me./ I am its legend." Guillén's poetic attitude is far removed from romantic subjectivity. He *depends on* things; the exterior reality *invents* him, he is its *legend*. Man, the "legend," is part of objective reality. *"Leyenda* is, as it were, the legend of man, but referred to here as subject to reality. As in a reciprocal relationship (*juego recíproco*). That which emphasizes the objective character of the real." (J.G.)

To express this personal and positive view of the world, the poet makes concrete images of abstractions; thus, "The soul / veers toward the eyes . . ." "I save the present." "I assemble . . . destiny" "To surge up in centuries, / to carry off Being." Guillén's poetry is of the present, the moment lived and enjoyed, of Being and Becoming; seldom of the past.

In the final stanza the poet says, *Soy, más, estoy . . .* which I have translated "I am; I am here and now." Spanish has two verbs for "to be": *ser* and *estar*. Guillén thus can express Being in the abstract (*ser*) and in the immediate and concrete (*estar*). The conciseness and fullness of this distinction cannot be expressed in English; the translator must paraphrase.

The form of the strophe is a quatrain with assonantal rhyme on the second and fourth lines. I have used a quatrain in translating, but with rhymes on the first and fourth. Assonantal rhyme—vowel rhyme—is difficult to use consistently in English, but it appears occasionally in this translation in such rhymes as "yields" and "real."

Los nombres. (The Names):

Here the Platonic Idea (the name, the eternal), is opposed to life, brief, swift and transitory, symbolized by the rose. It is true that the rose dies; but ... *quedan los nombres,* the names remain. Yet the poet is not a Platonist; what interests him is precisely that quality of transitoriness that the rose epitomizes: the passing moment. "May the instant's acrid / plunge lift us, move / us to unending love!" Life may be fleeting, a shadow; but let us, says the poet, live it deeply.

Manantial (The Source)

This poem is based on the metaphor spring-girl, and recalls the famous painting by Ingres called *La Source*. The water gradually takes form through the poem, until at last there emerges, "slender and curved," the figure of a girl.

Naturaleza viva (Unstill Life):

This poem illustrates Guillén's love for common, every-day objects—a chair, a window, here a table—a love shared by other contemporary poets, by Francis Ponge, William Carlos Williams, Pablo Neruda. The title is a pun on the expression *Naturaleza muerta* (literally "dead nature") which in Spanish means a "still life." Guillén has changed it to *Naturaleza viva*—nature alive —to indicate that the tabletop bears within it its past of tree and forest.

The poem moves from the common object—the walnut tabletop—to its abstraction, the *idea* of levelness and smoothness, in the third and fourth lines. However, the poet feels that for his own certainty he must touch and press the surface, to assure himself of his (and its) reality. The wood's feel and texture recall its origin: the walnut tree that produced it and the forest to which it belonged. The walnut and its history are present in its knots and grain, in its present physical reality; the power of the tree and the forest are concentrated in the smooth tabletop which will always hold within it the memory of the wilderness. The poem moves from a present physical reality (the walnut tabletop) to its abstraction (the idea of levelness) and then back to immediate reality. The last four lines combine these various ideas.

The translation of "Unstill Life" appeared in the *Northwest Review,* Vol. XVIII, No. 1 (Summer, 1966), pp. 61–63, under the title "Still Life."

ADVENIMIENTO (ADVENT):

An epiphany, a manifestation of timelessness in the beauty of a moment: its title suggests a miracle. *Arrebol* (reddish clouds) and *luna* speak of a sunrise. All is not lost; past happiness will return with the birds that sing "artlessly," without design. (These lines recall others by the great Golden Age poet Fray Luis de León:

> *Despiértenme las aves*
> *con su cantar sabroso no aprendido ...*
> (Let the birds awake me
> with their sweet unlearned song . . .)

Are those past times irrecoverable? the poet asks in the final stanza. Let us, he seems to reply, leave it to Chance, that fickle god.

SABOR A VIDA (LIFETASTE):

Sabor (like the English "savor") means "taste," but the title suggests a taste not of but *like* life: lifetaste. Breath, air, sky, and joy are mentioned in the first lines of *Sabor a vida;* all are major themes of Guillén's poetry, and they set the poem's mood of expanding intoxication with the sufficiency of the present. The poet floats through hazards and joys; "the joys deepen and scatter": the typical Guillenian metaphor that lends concrete qualities to abstractions. (The first two lines say literally: "There is a sky now in the air that is breathed.") Here the poet does not seek exotic pleasures; he finds his felicity in the familiar manifestations of nature: the sun, the shade, the air, the moment. (My alliteration of "hunting" and "hounded" is intended to suggest that of *caza* and *ca-cería*.) The Present, in the third strophe, is elusive in its pith and marrow; it rewards his loitering. Guillén's celebration of the Present, the moment, Becoming, has led some critics to point out his nexus with Existentialism, which emphasizes lived experience over abstractions. But Guillén is not an Existentialist poet, because he seems untroubled, in the poems of *Cántico,* by the anguish, the dread before nothingness, which are the concern of the Existentialists. His is a poetry not of Nothingness, but of Being, its fullness and immediacy. The finale is *fortissimo:* the poet is enjoying the sound of his own footsteps, perhaps relishing his own solitude (but *compañía* could refer to a friend or the beloved.) The present, the moment rises to an ecstatic intensity, and the poem ends with a meaningful inversion, where instead of *never possible glory* we see that Guillén means a "possibility of glory never abolished."

There are five quatrains, three of which have the alternate line short. The two quatrains of four full lines of eight syllables each (*octosílabos*) provide a movement that suggests strophe and antistrophe. The assonantal rhyme on the vowels *i* and *a* is maintained throughout.

This commentary by Julian Palley is from *The Poem Itself,* edited by Stanley Burnshaw. Copyright (c) 1960 by Stanley Burnshaw. Reprinted by permission of Holt, Rinehart and Winston, Inc.

Cima de la delicia (Summit of Delight):

Once again Guillén's familiar themes: the air, the mo-

187

ment, space, plenitude, light; and the use of abstractions made concrete ("The clearest distances / dream the true. . . ." "Toward the sun on wings / plenitude escapes.") The poem ascends to a fine intensity; yet in the fourth stanza it is clear that this discovery of beauty and fullness came late. But those "irreparable years" (the ones wasted) also have their charm in the present perspective.

PRIMAVERA DELGADA (SLENDER SPRING):

Primavera delgada is one of Guillén's most complex and successful poems. The title itself is a metaphor of an abstraction, the personification of a season: "Slender Spring." *Delgada,* like its English equivalent, suggests youth and rebirth. The personification conveys the image of the miracle of renascent nature on a spring day. The poem lyrically endows a moment with immortality. A simple event—boating on a river—is given transcendence by a series of metaphors involving river, sky, morning, poplars, oars and spring. These intricate metaphors are sometimes ambiguous in themselves and in their interrelation, but the ambiguity—a source of richness in poetry—sharpens the apprehension of an experience that is both dreamlike and permanent.

"Profileless space" (line one) is metaphorical because it indirectly bestows visual qualities upon space (a litotes: an indirect affirmation through negation). The cloud—which sums up the indecisive course of space—is symbolic of its lack of direction. The expression *a la deriva* (adrift) suggests the entire mood of the poem, that of a leisurely and carefree afternoon spent in communion with nature.

In the second and third couplets the river explores its bed, seeking its own denouement. The extended rivulets, part of the river's movement, are compared to an artist's strokes with brush or pencil that also "seek the conclusion" of a sketch or painting. In the fifth and sixth couplets, the deep opaque green of the water "denies its fish" to the observer above. In the seventh and eighth couplets, *lentas* is an adjective, modifying *alamedas,* but it has the force of an adverb. Yet our translation misses the suggestion of "slow poplar groves"—perhaps a vision of lethargically swaying trees. In these same verses morning is personified; moreover, the boat's wake helps it (the morning) conduct the river, suggested by the poplar groves, toward its destination. The river puts in tune, in harmony, the sky's undulation and the rhythmic oarstrokes, which themselves are metaphorically suggested by the word *pompas* (bubbles), leaving us with an image of a stream of bubbles created with each plunge of the oar. The poem ends with an apostrophe, evoking the vision of "slender spring" among the oars.

The series of clauses are connected by adverbial conjunctions (when, while) or prepositions (under, in favor of, with), the whole suggesting the river's leisurely movement, its "sinuous advance." The alternation of long and short verses conveys the feeling of rhythmic oarstrokes. The repetition of "when" and "while" seems to arrest time, affirming the supremacy of the moment. The delicate music of the assonantal rhyme, that intensifies the dreamlike quality of the verse, is untranslatable.

This commentary by Julian Palley is from *The Poem Itself*, edited by Stanley Burnshaw. Copyright (c) 1960 by Stanley Burnshaw. Reprinted by permission of Holt, Rinehart and Winston, Inc.

Desnudo (Nude):

Desnudo is a poem of a gradual emergence of things from the penumbra of a darkened room. It conveys, in precise and measured terms, an almost childlike wonder at the miracle and perfection of existence, and in this it resembles *Más allá* (discussed above). Guillén's being is dependent upon exterior reality, and in *Desnudo* this reality takes the form of a woman's body, a perfect creation, that emerges at first only in color (first stanza). The colors are "fugitive and mental," they are still almost abstract, ideas not yet coalesced into reality. The body's contour is hinted at only by "fugitive points of light"; chaos is still dominant. In the second stanza the color "consolidates itself into mass," and a vague form appears. The "pure and quiet profiles" (third stanza) annihilate the "base confusions." The poetry of *Cántico* celebrates the triumph of clarity; light, bright contours, tactile and visual certainty. Chaos is abhorred; only the clear outline of being is desired. In the fourth stanza the form (clear now) is a woman's body in repose. The physical presence of the beloved, the exactly "right monotone," is of prodigious intensity. The female body (last stanza) needs no *ambiente,* no atmosphere, no additional beauty, voice or flower, to set it off. It is its own realization. It is perfect not in its promise, but in its "absolute present."

Presencia, presente, plenitud inmediata: again the poet sings the moment, the *now*, its sufficiency and abundance.

The movement is slow, considered, measured. The eleven—and seven—syllable lines are frequently broken by pauses. The slow movement is intended to suggest the gradual appearance, to the eyes of the beholder, of the desired reality, the woman's body in its process of becoming.

This commentary by Julian Palley is from *The Poem Itself*, edited by Stanley Burnshaw. Copyright (c) 1960 by Stanley Burnshaw. Reprinted by permission of Holt, Rinehart and Winston, Inc.

Noche de luna (Moonlight night):

This enigmatic piece is suggestive in its ambiguity. Perhaps the entire poem is about *waiting, expectancy,* with the background of moonlight on water. A keen sense of something about to happen, an anticipation. (The expectancy is unresolved: "without denouement.") Several words here pertain to this experience: *veladora* (watchful), *vigía* (vigil), *la espera* (the waiting), *expectación* (expectation), *busca* (seek). The abstraction "cold" is materialized into a bird-metaphor in the fifth and sixth lines, where the "plumages of cold . . . soar." The fourth stanza is a provisional climax, as "the dreams of the algae . . . illuminate the night." The waiting is partly rewarded in this rare surrealist image. Then, as the dreams of the algae rise from the depths of the water, there is a general ascending, a movement upward in space ("The sands . . . demand grace of the wind") and in color ("ascension to white.") Along with the waiting-images, there are many words suggesting whiteness: *luz de luna* (moonlight), *candor* (candor), *plumajes de frío* (plumages of cold), *espuma* (foam), *lo blanco* (whiteness), *una blanca . . . ausencia* (a white . . . absence). The final question is Mallarméan in its seeming desire for whiteness and absence. There is no rhyme, but the seven-syllable line is maintained throughout.

ESTATUA ECUESTRE (EQUESTRIAN STATUE):

The *décima* or *espinela* is a ten line form, popular in the Spanish Golden Age, which usually rhymed ABBAACCDDC. Guillén here uses the French form of the *décima,* rhyming ABABCCDEED. The conciseness and symmetry of the form are well adapted to Guillén's vision of the world in *Cántico.*

There are many translations of this *décima,* and one of the best is by George Santayana. The poem's tension achieves a perfect balance between motion and stillness, the two opposing forces. The horse's "impulse," its "ambition to be far," is checked by the bronze of which it is made. The tension between motion and immobility invades the soul of the beholder.

MUERTE A LO LEJOS (DEATH IN THE DISTANCE):

This sonnet is a meditation on death, on death's meaning as part of the order of the universe, and a statement of the poet's attitude regarding the inevitable. Just as Guillén affirms life in all of its manifestations, he accepts the fact of his individual and inevitable death as a part of the life process. A suggestive paradox opens the poem: "At times I am troubled by a certainty." One is usually troubled by doubts or fears, by *uncertainties:* the certainty, of course, is that of his own death. "And there before me trembles my future": he is not afraid, he does not tremble. But his future (death) trembles before his eyes: the reaction usually inspired by the object is transferred to the object itself, thereby softening the image of fear. In lines two and three death suddenly assumes a more concrete form: a cemetery wall in a city suburb; the wall, in fact, that Guillén remembers from his childhood in Valladolid. The poet sees himself buried within those walls. Yet death's terror is softened by the presence —also inescapable—of sunlight and countryside. In lines four and five the poet asks if the image of death—the loss of light, forms, love—should inspire sadness. He replies that there is no need to dwell on it yet, because: "What is urgent is the ripe / fruit that the hand already peels." What deserves the concentration of our being is life in its infinite variety: knowledge, love, nature, art, the keen presence of the moment; there is too much to learn, to see, to hear, to touch; our lifetime is a moment, why waste it contemplating the *after*life, the unknown and unknowable? Better enjoy the fruit that the hand "now peels."

"And that will be the most sad / among days. Then let the hand offer and fall / without despair . . ." But the image remains, as it should, of our death, the "saddest day." The poet refuses to dwell on it morbidly, but neither will he blindly deny it. Light implies dark, birth implies death. It is part of the scheme of the universe;

one depends on the other, and a joyful acceptance of birth and light assumes the acceptance of their cycle and conclusion. "The hand should offer and fall without despair." He will not resist; there should be a calm yielding to necessity, symbolized by the hand's quiet gesture. These lines recall the great "Coplas a la muerte de su padre" of the fifteenth century poet Jorge Manrique, as well as certain sonnets of the Baroque poet Francisco de Quevedo, as E. M. Wilson and Hugo Montes have pointed out. Guillén's sonnet is in the Castilian tradition of serenity, clarity and resignation in the face of death.

194

"When death comes," says the poet in the last four lines, "I will accept it without tears: because it is just; because there is no preference, and all men suffer it equally; and above all, because it is part of the law of the universe. It is not an accident; it is not capricious or gratuitous; it is inevitable and right, part of the world's symmetry." That symmetry may be fearful, but more fearful still would be no rest, no end. The poet then faces the inevitable, like Jorge Manrique, *con voluntad placentera:* with serene accord.

This commentary by Julian Palley is from *The Poem Itself,* edited by Stanley Burnshaw. Copyright (c) 1960 by Stanley Burnshaw. Reprinted by permission of Holt, Rinehart and Winston, Inc.

The translation "Death in the Distance," appeared in the *Colorado Quarterly,* Vol. V, No. 2 (Autumn, 1956), p. 138.

Esos cerros (The Hills):

The first two words are examples of what the Spanish critic Bousoño calls "rational suggestion," where an idea is compressed into a single word, a device used frequently by Guillén. Perhaps the poem yields its meaning thus: Do you want purity and solitude? Well, they are there in the grey of those hills. They are perfect and untouched: the most wayward foot has not trod them. Beyond them stretches oblivion, nothing, a Nothing (and here it is personified) that is almost visible, waiting to take form. Yet the poet feels compassion for this Nothing: the air shelters it. The nothingness wants to be, and the perfect greys protect it in its vigil. The poem is suffused by grey, which exists beside, and almost fades into, Nothingness.

Los jardines (The Gardens):

In "The Gardens," the poet looks back on his childhood. But Time, which he sees in retrospect and in perspective, becomes one with the present moment: "What transparence of many afternoons, forever joined!" The past and the present exist simultaneously.

Más vida (More life):

This poem is both about parenthood—its wonder, joys and perplexities—and the miracle of creation that manifests itself in the flow of human life, a flow viewed as a continuous fire, the sparks of which are individual lives. To creation in the abstract and in the concrete (his son) he directs his *salve!* or "hail!"

(PART VI) Jorge Guillén explains that his use of the word *ángel* is broad enough to include both the idea of the traditional semi-deity, and that implied by the Andalusian expression *tener ángel,* which means to have a special, almost magic charm or wit.

(PART VII) A vision of his son together with nature, the youthful and "hopeful" air of June. The June air is an "ambush" in that it lies in wait for the miraculous; *a la gracia dispuesto,* "ready for the touch of grace": "grace" is perhaps used here in the religious sense, the presence of the divine.

(PART IX) "Errors with sorrows / Disasters . . ." A recognition of the anguish and doubt that accompanies human life; all is not wonder and discovery. But even with its "wars of Cain" life is worth the undertaking. Creation now passes on to his son, who will fashion his own future.

LA SALIDA (THE SALLY):

"It is the act of rushing into the sea, with its glories and lights, its foam and soft spray." (J.G.)

CALLEJEO (CALLEJEO):

I have retained the original Spanish title because I can't find an equivalent for it. *Callejeo* is formed from *calle,* "street." I suppose the closest approximation would be "Walking Around," or better, "Walking Around Streets."

PART II

In Part II, poems from "All Men, or Almost"

("*Todos o casi todos los hombres*") through "Writing on the Wall" ("*Pared*") are from *Maremágnum*. Poems from "Ant Alone" ("*Hormiga sola*") through "Deer on a Wall" ("*Ciervos sobre una pared*") are from *Que van a dar en la mar*. "Clover Leaves" ("*Tréboles*") is from *Maremágnum* and *A la altura de las circunstancias*. Poems from "Spanish Awakening" ("*Despertar español*") through "Shattered Clamor" ("*Clamor estrellado*") are from *A la altura de las circunstancias*.

Todos o casi todos los hombres (All Men or Almost):

The poet here laments the present tendency to consider human lives as things, as commodities to be manipulated, whether by statesmen, generals, actuaries, or by the gentlemen of the "think factories," the Rand Corporations, who are calmly deciding how many of us will have to be sacrificed in case of nuclear warfare. Human life is, or should be, sacred.

Dafne a medias (Half-way Daphne):

According to the poet, he here satirizes those immigrants who would break entirely with their European past, and become totally "Americanized." The speaker does not reflect the poet's ideas; on the contrary, Guillén elsewhere affirms his confidence in the future of Spain and Europe (see "Spanish Awakening").

Los atracadores (The Hold-up Men):

"Threads of novels tied together": that is, the "more or

less subtle relation between the more or less novelistic lives of those who pass through the hotel." (J.G.)

In this poem the objective of the criminals—money and the "good life"—is seen as no different from that of respectable citizens. Only their means of attaining it differs, in this criticism of American materialism.

EL ENGAÑO A LOS OJOS (THE EYES' DECEIT):

The form of the original is a *romance,* a ballad consisting of eight-syllable lines with alternating assonantal rhyme in *a-o.* It is a vision of youth under a modern dictatorship, rebellious and proud, enjoying a spurious freedom, really controlled and directed by their elders. The title derives from a major theme of *Don Quijote*: that of the difficulty of distinguishing illusion from reality, and was the title of a play envisioned, though perhaps never completed, by Cervantes. The poem "Los hijos," (The Sons) also from *Maremágnum,* is a recognition (in a sense, a reply to this poem) of the valor of those young people who have now dared to challenge the dictatorship.

AIRE CON ÉPOCA (AIR OF OUR TIME):

The air, which was a major *motif* of *Cántico,* appears again, but in a different context. In *Cántico* it is a symbol of the enveloping world, of which Guillén feels himself a part; through it, he communes with, and exalts in, nature. In *Aire con época,* however, the air "transmits to us / the minute's history," it conveys, on all sides, a message of man's ascendance over nature, the overwhelming power of scientific expansion, which may turn, in the end, against him. But Guillén does not despair. As he states toward the end of the poem: "I hope. Every affirmation affirms me."

CIERVOS SOBRE UNA PARED (DEER ON A WALL):

Lascaux is, of course, the cave in southern France famous for its prehistoric wall paintings.

In an effort to preserve the terseness of the original, I have used mostly six-syllable lines in translating Guillén's nine-syllable verses. My version has twenty-seven lines. The original, which has alternating assonantal rhyme in *e–a,* has twenty-four.

TRÉBOLES (TRÉBOLES):

Tréboles, or "clover leaves," is the name Guillén gives to these short, pithy, sometimes humorous verses; the rich gnomic tradition in Spanish, beautifully cultivated in this century by Antonio Machado among others, goes back to Rabbi Sem Tob in the fourteenth century. These are a few examples of the many *tréboles* that appear in *Clamor.*

No. 1 is from *Maremágnum;* the rest are from *A la altura de las circunstancias.*

DESPERTAR ESPAÑOL (SPANISH AWAKENING):

Once more a poem of "awakening," but now with broader implications: the desired, future awakening of the nation. Compare this with: "Half-way Daphne." There is no attempt here to cut off European roots; his Spanish origin, and his adherence to the tradition, are passionately affirmed.

(PART I): Language is the key to culture and tradition. The poet is alone, an exile, cut off from his milieu; but the words—his Spanish words—accompany him and return to him his past. Through language man can aspire to authentic humanity.

(PART II) A looking backward to his country's past mistakes and forward to a possible future. The "air" and "light" of *Cántico*: "fresh new voices . . . will resound toward other airs," and "an antique light . . . that will kindle the eyes of other men / perhaps, and their discoveries." (There is no sufficient English equivalent for the word *hallazgos*. It can mean discovery, finding, invention, perception, but it is stronger than any of these words, nearly all of which have technical associations. "Discovery," of course, in a Spanish context, has unwanted connotations for American readers.)

(PART III) "A flowing"—that of language, culture, history—is never ending, never "runs down to the sea." (An allusion to the *Coplas* of Jorge Manrique: "Our lives are rivers / that run down to the sea . . .") The future will be the work of our free will. The Spanish tradition is "permanence" and "change."

(PART IV) Spain is "captivating amid sculpting hands," that is, superb in its artistic endeavors, but "never beneath hatreds," discouraging in its history of social and religious conflicts.

(PART V) The "white wall," Lorca's symbol for Spain. *¡Durase junto al muro!* (May I remain beside that wall!), an unusual use of the past subjunctive. With reference to this passage, the poet recalls a verse of Fray

Luis de León (1527–91), which, he says, may be its "source":

> . . . ¡oh *dulce olvido!*
> ¡*durase en tu reposo . . . !*

> (. . . Oh sweet forgetfulness!
> May I remain in your repose . . .)

> from his *Oda a Salinas*

CLAMOR ESTRELLADO (SHATTERED CLAMOR):

This, the final poem of *Clamor,* closes its three volumes, in which the most persistent note is one of outcry against man's folly: dictatorship, injustice, discrimination, the threat of nuclear destruction, the excesses of technology and materialism. Finally the poet's sight turns toward the stars and space, and again man's history is seen *sub specie aeternitatis.* The word *estrellado* means "spangled with stars, shattered or smashed," and its root is *estrella,* "star." So the title contains the double idea of "an end to clamor" and "man's clamor seen from the viewpoint of the stars."

Works of Jorge Guillén

Cántico (Fe de vida). First edition, Madrid, Revista de Occidente, 1928; second edition, Madrid, Cruz y Raya, 1936; third edition, Mexico, Litoral, 1945; fourth edition (Primera edición completa), Buenos Aires, Editorial Sudamericana, 1950.

Ardor. Paris, Manuel Altolaguirre, 1931.

El encanto de las sirenas. Mexico, 1953.

Huerto de Melibea. Madrid, Insula, 1954.

Del amanecer y el despertar. Valladolid, 1956.

Luzbel desconcertado. Milan, 1956.

Lugar de Lázaro. Málaga, 1957.

The last five poems appear in the first two parts of *Clamor*.

Clamor, I, *Maremágnum*. Buenos Aires, Editorial Sudamericana, 1957.

Viviendo y otros poemas. Barcelona, Seix Barral, 1958.

Federico en persona. Buenos Aires, EMECE, 1959.

Historia natural. Breve antología con versos inéditos. Palma de Mallorca, Papeles de Son Armadans, 1960.

Clamor, II, . . . *Que van a dar en la mar*. Buenos Aires, Sudamericana, 1960.

Language and Poetry. Cambridge, Harvard University Press, 1961.

El argumento de la obra. Milan, Scheiwiller, 1961.

Lenguaje y poesía. Madrid, 1962.

Clamor, III, *A la altura de las circunstancias*. Buenos Aires, 1963.

Tréboles. Santander, 1964.

Selección de poemas. Madrid, 1965.

Cántico: A Selection. Edited by Norman Thomas di
    Giovanni. Boston, 1965.
Homenaje. Milan, Scheiwiller, 1967.
Aire nuestro. Milan, Scheiwiller, 1968.

Selected Bibliography

Alonso, Dámaso. *Poetas españoles contemporáneos.* Madrid, 1953. Pages 235–43.

Burnshaw, Stanley, ed. *The Poem Itself,* New York, 1960. Commentaries by Julian Palley on "Desnudo," "Sabor a vida," "Muerte a lo lejos," and "Primavera delgada." Pages 210–17.

Casalduero, Joaquín. *Cántico de Jorge Guillén.* Madrid, 1953.

Castro, Américo. "Cántico de Jorge Guillén," *Insula,* Vol. I, No. 1 (1943), 14–27.

Ciplijauskaité, Biruté. *"Clamor* a la altura de las circunstancias," *Revista Hispánica Moderna,* Vol. XXIX (1963), 290–93.

Darmangeat, Pierre. *Jorge Guillén ou le Cantique émerveillé.* Paris, 1958.

Debicki, Andrew P. "Jorge Guillén's *Cántico,"* PMLA, Vol. LXXXI, No. 5 (1966), 439–45.

Florit, Eugenio. "Notas sobre la poesía de Jorge Guillén," *Revista Hispánica Moderna,* Vol. XII (1946), 267–71.

Gil de Biedma, Jaime. *Cántico: El mundo y la poesía de Jorge Guillén.* Barcelona, 1960.

González Muela, Joaquín. *La realidad y Jorge Guillén.* Madrid, 1962.

Gullón, Ricardo, and José Manuel Blecua. *La poesía de Jorge Guillén.* Zaragoza, 1949.

Ivask, Ivar, ed. "An International Symposium in Honor of Jorge Guillén at 75," *Books Abroad,* Vol. 42, No. 1 (Winter, 1968), 7–60.

MacLeish, Archibald. "Jorge Guillén: A Poet of This Time," *Atlantic Monthly* (January, 1961), 127–29.

Palley, Julian. "The Metaphors of Jorge Guillén," *Hispania,* Vol. XXXVI, No. 3 (1953), 321–24.

———. "Jorge Guillén and the Poetry of Commitment," *Hispania,* Vol. XLV, No. 4 (1962), 686–91.

Pleak, Frances A. *The Poetry of Jorge Guillén.* Princeton, 1942.

Salinas, Pedro. *Literatura española siglo XX.* Mexico, 1941. Pages 263–76.

Vivanco, Luis Felipe. *Introducción a la poesía española contemporánea.* Madrid, 1957. Pages 88–92.

Weber, Robert J. "De *Cántico* a *Clamor,*" *Revista Hispánica Moderna,* Vol. XXIX (1963), 109–19.

Zardoya, Concha. *Poesía española contemporánea.* Madrid, 1961. Pages 288–90.